WOMANISH...
CONFESSIONS

Angelia Vernon MENCHAN

M&AMenchanMedia 2020

Living with Our Choices
Audra Confesses

*I never found Maynard especially attractive.
Audre thought. He was only two inches taller than
me, kind of chubby, though he claimed to always
be working on it and light skin wasn't my thing.
But when I met him I had two kids under seven and
though I had a better than average job working as
a buyer for a major retail chain, I was almost
thirty and tired.*

*I graduated with an Associate's Degree in
retail management at twenty and got a decent job
as a department manager at the same company I
currently worked for and was able to move in an
apartment and get a car. But by twenty-five I had
two kids for two men, neither of whom provided
much other than good penis. They were tall, dark
and fit and my type. But they also both still lived at
home with their mamas and had other babies. Me
and the women were all digging for rubbish in an
almost empty can. I made a decision that by thirty
I would be married, in a home and pregnant with
child number three from my husband.*

Audre met Maynard on the day he started
working. He was the newest management hire and
the company made a big deal with those,
especially if he or she were Black. There was
coffee, pastries and an exuberant introduction.

Audre wasn't a manager but was lead buyer for the past three years in women and children's clothing. Audre zoomed in on Maynard noting his trendy suit that was made to make the best of his bulk. There was also an air of confidence about him that she saw in many professional, educated Black men. That, *I Am the Ish.* It showed in the way they stood, spoke and faced the crowd. But she also knew from living that it was born from the pain of early rejection because they were too short, fat or nerdy. Their education and or money had bought the confidence. It was 2010 and she knew Maynard was earning six figures, easily more than triple her fifty thousand. Her eyes focused on him as he spoke.

"Thanks everyone for the welcome. I'm Maynard Griffin and I've been with the company five years. I graduated from Morehouse in 1993 and spent twelve years in banking before transitioning. This company has provided me opportunities and allowed me to give more opportunities. I'm glad to be part of your team." He glanced around, making sure he met everyone's eyes.

Audre stood, clapping, encouraging others to do likewise. She knew Maynard's eyes would zoom in on her. She was taller than average with an amazing figure encased in a well-fitting dress in jade. Her shoulder length auburn hair complemented her medium brown complexion and her makeup was flawless. Her appearance was important to her and she worked on it. Her mother Lois taught her that early and often. Maynard's eyes raked over her completely before thanking the crowd. She smiled at him slightly before looking away. She was the kind of woman who usually never looked his way.

After the speech many stood to greet him but Audre sat in her chair, perusing her phone.

"That must be intriguing." Maynard said. Audre glanced up to him standing over her. The scent of cologne and sweat filled her nostrils. *It is too hot for all those clothes.* Audre thought. *That's why he's sweating.*

"Not at all. I'm working on several orders that must be done today." Pushing her chair back a bit, Audre stood, closing her phone.

"I'm Audre Childress; I'm a buyer for children and women." Maynard smiled, offering his hand that she lightly shook.

"I hear you're *the buyer*. It's nice to meet you. I'm glad you don't work under my leadership." Audre's brow lifted at his words.

"Why is that Maynard Griffin?"

"Because the rules say managers can't fraternize with those under their leadership."

"And you want to fraternize with me?" Audre's hip was jutted a bit to the side as she threw back her head allowing her hair to move sensually. Maynard watched her, biting into his bottom lip.

"Perhaps. We will talk soon." He said, walking away.

Those memories filled Audra's head as she left Derrick's house. Derrick was her second lover since marrying Maynard in 2011 and the one she was falling in love with. The thing though was Derrick offered great sex, humorous and enlightening conversation but he earned a teacher's salary and lived in a fixer upper in the hood. He wasn't an option for longevity. Maynard was. His salary had more than doubled in eight years and her kids, Marlon and Marvin at sixteen and fourteen considered him Dad. They also had a little girl, Marilyn, aged seven who was Maynard's heart. She loved the *life* Maynard provided and loved him as her husband and father of her child but had grown to avoid his touch. He was a mediocre lover at best who refused to experiment beyond intercourse and perfunctory oral sex on his part but wanted her to perform it for him regularly.

That had become their staple. She provided oral, he came quickly and they went on with their lives. But Derrick was becoming too much and she needed to tear herself away but she needed to see her mentor/therapist.

SCENE TWO

Ms. Ann's space was always serene and smelled of flowers and herbs. Audre met her when she was a senior in high school trying to get into the local college. Audre was hard working and loved fashion but had never been better than a C+ student and that was with effort. She loved reading but math and science was always a challenge and she hated history. She had focused on classes she had to take and filled her slate with classes she could master such as clothing, cooking and drama classes. Jacksonville offered curriculum in magnet schools that met her needs and brought up her less than good grades in math, science and history, thus her C+ status. She loved fashion, dressing and was a great cook, her maternal grandmother Pearl Davis had ensured that. Lois taught her to sew and how to wear clothes and makeup. Lois worked as a cafeteria aide all her life but dressed to impress and did the same for her only child.

Ms. Ann's organization *You Are More Than Average* offered scholarships to students with 2.0 to 2.9 grade point averages. The premise was to get an associate's degree in a field that supported better than minimum wages. The criteria also included not having any children and the ability to focus on your studies for two years. The program paid all expenses for education, books and there was a small stipend. Audre recalled asking Ms.

Ann why scholarships for average students. The tall, imposing woman with deep-set eyes and a soft deep voice had chuckled at the question before answering.

"Because no one else offers it love. I feel if you made the effort and have a desire to get minimally an associate's degree, why can't assist with that? Students with B and above average have a plethora of scholarships, there is money for single mothers, formerly incarcerated people and the list goes on. I feel if one maintained a C average with hard work why not assist them.

Audre loved that answer and grew to love the woman. When she got pregnant at twenty two and twenty four there was no judgment just guidance to programs to assist with childcare while she worked. Pearl was in heaven and Lois in her forties at the time. Lois made it clear she had raised her child. There was never a time when Ms. Ann hadn't mentored or counseled her since they met. She was now in her early sixties and retired yet she still *talked* to many of the young women she mentored, counseled or assisted in getting educated. She had a small place downtown where she met with them because her husband respected what she did but insisted it was less than twenty hours per week and not in their residence. The place was a small home converted to a sanctuary.

Occasionally there were young women residing there temporarily.

"Hey Ms. Ann." Audre said as the elder enveloped her in an embrace.

"Hello Audre, would you like a drink or food?"

There was always food and beverages offered.

"No ma'am." Audre just wanted to confess to her mentor. Ms. Ann knew about her previous affair that was very brief but had no idea of the month's long sexual liaison with Derrick. But after what happened the day before she had to tell her.

"Ms. Ann, I'm in trouble, again." Audre confessed, looking into the eyes of her mentor but as usual couldn't read her. "I've been having an affair for more than a year and I love him... crave him. I tried breaking it off but showed up at his house yesterday and created a scene. A woman was there and I went berserk as if I didn't have a husband or kids. It turns out the woman was his relative. I'm horrified, I could have been arrested or something." Ann picked up the glass of lemon water and took a sip. Her eyes remained on Audre who was starting to fidget. After quenching her thirst, Ann placed the glass on the table and patted her lips dry.

"Is your biggest concern that you could have been arrested Audre?"

Audre flinched. She hated when Ms. Ann said her name when addressing her. The question also felt weighted.

"That's a big deal. I mean Maynard and the kids finding out would be part of that but still." Audra knew how selfish that sounded but she always felt truthful with Ms. Ann even when she didn't come out in a good light.

"Is the fact you're having another affair when you're married to a good man not a big concern? I don't know Maynard as well as I know you but I know he loves you." There wasn't a hint of judgment or censure in the words. The woman simply asked questions allowing the recipient to answer. She stated her feelings just as dispassionately.

"It is... Ms. Ann, I love Maynard but he's an unconcerned lover. He takes five minutes to kiss me, twist my nipples too hard and ejaculate inside me. If he performs oral and I don't come in five minutes then he stops. I'm thirty nine..." Ms. Ann steepled her fingers.

"With needs... I understand that but you knew Maynard's lovemaking style before marrying him.

You decided sex was less important than marrying a well-paid man, moving to Marsh Landing and getting to spend your considerable pay as you choose. That my dear was your choice and trade off."

Audra popped out of her chair and walked to the kitchen, retrieving a bottle of blackberry flavored water. She placed it on her forehead, allowing Ms. Ann's last statement to roll around in her head. It was the truth. To have the life she wanted she had done what she said she would, find a man with money who loved her more than she loved him. At the time she thought she could just please herself and deal with it. But four years in she had a brief sexual fling but this thing with Derrick was something else. She stayed too long and fell in love with the sex and him. Derrick was Marvin's soccer coach in addition to being his civics teacher. She had allowed a little flirting to turn into a full-fledged affair with drama. The night before Derrick had thrown her out and told her to not return. For him, she was a fling. She opened the water and walked back into the room and dropped into her chair. Ms. Ann sat calmly waiting.

"You're right, of course Ms. Ann but it's horrible. I want to cry when he touches me. I tried to tell him how to please me but he got offended. Now he's quite mean sometimes."

"I'm not sure what you're calling mean but I'm sure he's hurt and hurt people strike out. He might even suspect you of something. Most people who are cheated on are aware in their own way Audra. It allows him to have his dignity. Does this new man love you?" A snort of derision escaped Audra.

"Of course not; I'm married and he knows I'm not leaving Maynard for him. I was fun. He's my son's coach and teacher."

"That's very close to home." Ann said.

"It is but I rarely go to games or practice. I met him last year during a four week period when Maynard was opening a new store in California. I haven't been to a game or the school since. Marvin is an excellent student and Maynard attends all his and Marlon's events and stuff. He took them over after we married. I go with Marilyn. It's been great for the boys. Maynard didn't father them but he's their dad. They met him at eight and six. He's great with them. To him Derrick is a nobody who coaches his kids." Audra said with disdain not realizing that's exactly how she felt about Derrick though she had fallen in love with him.

"Does Maynard think you're a nobody Audre?" Ann asked softly. Audre's eyes filled and she rubbed the tears away quickly.

"He sort of does. He never says it like that but periodically reminds me he earns 300 to my 60 and of my *little* degree. He never said that until we were married and long before I had an affair. I met his parents, right before we got engaged. They both have advanced degrees, he told them I purchased clothes for a living and earned a nice little salary. Mrs. Griffin asked what school I attended and Maynard quickly told her a technical school. I'm proud of my degree. Fortunately they live in California and I don't see them often. They don't approve of me but their son had to have me. They also adore Marilyn and are kind to my boys."

Ann knew that story too well. Men who fell in love and married women with less education, money and jobs. She knew it was often because he was insecure and felt women who were equal in those areas wouldn't choose them. Traditionally men often married what they were now calling *down*. A term Ann didn't like but with women often out earning men in the past ten years or more the tides had turned thus the creation of the term. She suspected Derrick likely earned as much as Audre, if not more but nowhere near what Maynard earned. Maynard was now a general manager and opened new stores around the country.

"Why did he have to have you Audre?"

"I'm pretty; fine with great teeth and all this hair is mine. I may not be as educated but..." Audra said drily fluffing up her thick, beautifully relaxed hair. Ann chuckled but knew it to be true. Men had often commented on her thick, natural curls, complexion and curves as being a great commodity. "There was also another manager who was after me when Maynard arrived. He was biracial and I was even less attracted to him. Maynard was my catch and I guess poor sex and a bit of derision became my portion." Audre suddenly sounded sad and tired. She and Ann knew, poor sex and derision would not make Audre leave Maynard and she suspected a little sex on the side wouldn't make Maynard leave his prize. Weaker marriages were built on less.

"Thanks Ms. Ann, I always feel better if a little banged up after talking to you."

"I wouldn't be doing what I'm called to do if I didn't bang you up a bit. Just remember we live with the choices we make. And the only way from a bad choice is out."

~~YYYYY~~

Maynard embraced Audre, looking into her eyes when she arrived home. The boys were doing homework and Marilyn was playing sous chef to her daddy. He didn't cook often because Audre was a great cook but he was great at steak, his special potato dish with cheese and onions and mixed vegetables. Marilyn was cutting cheese with a butter knife. The marble counter was full of vegetables. Audre was going to bring takeout but she called and Maynard said he would cook. He worked ten to twelve hours most days but was off at three on Fridays. Audra didn't work on Fridays. On Thursdays she worked late but that was when she was usually with Derrick a few hours.

"Are you good? How is Ms. Ann?" He asked, allowing Marilyn to squeeze in and hug her mom before racing back to her tasks.

"I'm good just a little tired. Thanks for cooking." She said, allowing his embrace. "Ms. Ann is good. It's hard to believe she's in her sixties though."

"I agree. She's a good looking woman but a little too insightful looking for me." Laughter spilled from Audra. She believed him because insightful looking was an understatement. The woman looked as if she saw your damn soul. Maynard chuckled with her. "Marilyn, I'm going to talk to your mom a bit, go wash up." Marilyn quickly raced from the room. Audre sat at the bar and Maynard handed her a glass of wine. Nervous energy filled her belly.

"What's up?" She asked. Maynard stood on the other side of the bar. He was wearing an open throat white button down shirt and khaki slacks, his idea of dressing down. There wasn't a spot on his clothing though he had steak sizzling, potatoes peeled and vegetables chopped. He was still chubby but always immaculate.

"Miami called me today. They offered me the whole southern district. It's only slightly bigger but the money is ridiculous. You can keep your job and work remotely." He sounded thrilled. Audre knew it was a possibility down the road but Maynard presented it as a long shot months earlier. In short order, Audra realized this was a way out of her mess and wondered if Ms. Ann prayed it. She was convinced the woman had super powers. She smiled genuinely and saw his shoulders relax. Maynard's shoulders went up when he was unsure. She would never share she noticed that with him. To everyone, including her mom, Ms. Ann being the exception, she painted him as perfect. She never mentioned him to Derrick.

"Maynard, that's awesome. How soon?"

"Soon. The kids are out of school in six weeks and they are offering a home buyout the way the feds do. They pay us the market value of the home and then sell it. That means we can get whatever you want in Miami. I'm excited. I think you... we need this as a family."

Her heart leapt in her throat as she wondered how much Maynard knew. Because as her grandma used to say, 'She showed her ass' at Derrick's the night before. It wouldn't shock her if Derrick hadn't called him. She had yelled, cussed, hit and finally cried. Derrick's cousin rolled out threatening to kick her behind if she weren't so crazy and Derrick threw her out threatening to call the cops. She had driven around until she calmed down and was glad to find Marilyn in bed and the boys and Maynard watching a game when she arrived home. She quickly showered took a sedative and went to bed.

"That's great. I was thinking of going back to school and getting my bachelors. If not now, when?" Maynard beamed, he tried getting her to do that for years. She had savings from her earnings and Maynard took care of all household bills and placed money in her account for incidentals. She knew they would purchase their home out right. She wanted to cry at all she risked but was a master at hiding her feelings.

"I'm with that. It's a new start for all of us. Marlon doesn't even mind doing his junior and senior year at a new school. Especially, since he wants to go to the University of Miami." It bothered her he talked to the boys before her but she sucked it down. This was as good for them as for her. She also knew Maynard loved having the boys on his side if she didn't want to do something.

"How soon is dinner, I want to change?" She asked.

"Thirty minutes."

Standing in the shower she allowed the hot water to cascade down on her. She knew she was given a reprieve and a choice to make before altering her life forever. She felt grateful and resigned. As Ms. Ann said, "Just remember we live with the choices we make. And the only way from a bad choice is out."

Out wasn't an option.

SCENE THREE

A week before leaving Audra invited Ann to lunch. She hadn't seen Derrick in that time and focused on preparing to move, getting the kids and her registered for school and purchasing a new home. What she didn't know was Maynard called Ann for advice the week after telling her about the move. Ann thought about it as she got dressed for lunch.

Hello Ms. Ann this is Maynard Griffin. How are you?" Ann had met Maynard on several occasions. He donated to her ministry and attended her events with Audra. He even served on a couple of boards with her and they were cordial at best. Her husband, a retired military officer and professor considered him a pompous tight ass. She didn't disagree but he had never phoned her.

"I'm well. How are you, is Audra okay?"

"She's good. I just wanted your advice. I've taken a new job in Miami and Audra seems thrilled but sometimes I seem to not know my wife as well as you might. Do you think this is a great move? The kids are thrilled." Clarity filled Ann. Maynard was feeling disconnected from his wife and made a big

play by moving the family. He was now second guessing himself and needed reassurance.

"Maynard if she seems thrilled, then I would assume she's thrilled. She hasn't mentioned the move to me but her being thrilled and the kids being thrilled seems like a win. Are you thrilled Maynard?" He ran his hand over his head, feeling lulled by her deep, soothing voice.

"I am. We need this move, Audra and I. The kids are easygoing and well rounded. Marlon is especially thrilled because the U is his first choice in colleges. Ms. Ann, I want what's best for my family, mainly my wife." She heard the love and concern in his voice but bit her tongue to not say, then get sex counseling but she would never betray Audra or what she said in confidence. She suspected Maynard likely thought he was a great lover. Some men thought all they needed to bring to the game was an erection.

"I pray your move is great for all of you. Be well."

Ann hadn't given him anything concrete but he felt better for the conversation. She was told that was one of her gifts.

Ann watched Audre sashay in, her hair cut to a swingy bob and colored dark blonde. She looked stunning and serene. Her curves were encased in a pale pink fitted sheath and eyes followed her to the table. Ann stood to hug her. It had been two months since their last meeting which was about average. They ordered before Audra filled her in on the move. Ann always allowed her mentees to lead conversations.

"That's great." Ann said. "Does Derrick know?" Audre gasped in shock. Ms. Ann sometimes was a gut puncher.

"I haven't seen Derrick. Maynard told me about the job the same day I spoke to you. I've been getting things ready. I'm going back to college. Ms. Ann, you really bring the zingers sometimes." Ann lifted her shoulders in a shrug.

"It's a fair question Audre. Two months ago you were crying in your blackberry water and saying you loved Derrick. Now you're swinging your hair and hips. Unresolved shit is still shit." Audra snorted and started laughing, almost hysterically. Ann watched her and handed her a napkin once she stopped. Tears rained down her face.

"Oh my god… Ms. Ann that sounds so bad." Ann shrugged again.

"Truth often does. Audre you can run but the sex with Maynard is still what it is. Unless he gets sex counseling or you get spayed or neutered, I always forget which is which; sooner or later it's another lover or something." Audre knew the gloves were off. Ms. Ann didn't transition as much as glide into different modes. There was still not a tinge of judgment or correction. She simply stated her observations.

"Ms. Ann, we... yes I know. The sex isn't better but there is also not much of it. It was four years before the first affair and three before the next one. I'm not an oversexed hoochie." Ann leaned across the table.

"Audre, it's even worse, you're married and sexually unsatisfied. More so, you know what great, blow your back out sex is like. So it might only take two years this time." Audre's mouth opened and closed as she tried to gather her thoughts. She had nothing. Ms. Ann had read her and was right.

"Audre you and Maynard need counseling and sooner rather later. The new city, new house and college will wear off and then what? Also college is full of fine and willing men."

Audre blinked rapidly but only said, yes ma'am. Ms. Ann focused on her food; she said what she came to say.

Afterword Ms. Ann

I didn't see Audre for more than a year after they moved though I received periodic texts about school and how well the kids were doing. She knew I loved tea, candles and taffy so she sent gift boxes periodically but no calls. I don't call mentees after they break off contact unless I *feel* or hear *they* are in trouble or they ask for a call. There are far too many and it's intrusive. Many receive what they want or need from the connection and I allow that.

About sixteen months after I last saw her, I was in St. Augustine at Flagler College speaking and afterwards I was walking around downtown and spotted Audre as lovely as ever walking with a man who appeared to be in his late thirties. He was much taller than her, lean and muscular with dark chocolate skin, a beard and was dressed in a suit jacket, button down shirt and jeans. I knew immediately it was Derrick. I considered walking across the street to avoid them but decided against it. They were walking so close together their arms touched. I knew the minute Audre saw me, I was a few steps away and her eyes widened and she stumbled. He caught her and I saw her paste a smile on her face.

"Oh god, Ms. Ann, you startled me." She said. They stood in front of me, all of us blocking the sidewalk but there were no other walkers.

"Hello Audre. We should never be startled by friendly faces." Derrick looked on in interest, the smile on his face reaching his eyes. He was a beautiful man.

"Of course; I just didn't expect to see you here." Audra was clearly uncomfortable.

"Why not, I live fifty miles away, you're the surprise; Miami is a five hour drive."

"I know. I'm working again part-time and am here on a buying trip."

"Ah. Young man, I'm Ann Mitchell." I said offering my hand which he took and shook firmly. He grinned showing perfect teeth. Whew.

"Ma'am, I'm Derrick Allen. I know exactly who you are. Professor Mitchell is your husband and you're a legend. It's great to meet you."

Audre looked as if she wanted to flee.

"I'm sorry, where are my manners. Derrick, I've known Ms. Ann since I was eighteen, she helped me get into college and has mentored me on and off for twenty three years. Ms. Ann, Derrick is a friend and used to coach my son." I nodded focused on her. I wasn't going to make the encounter any easier.

"How is your family?" I finally asked.

"Everyone is great." She said.

"Great." I said and walked around them and on to the local tea shop. Once I was seated I saw a missed call but didn't respond or call her back. I needed more of a break from Audre and her life. I wanted two cups of lemongrass tea and a lemon cream scone.

AUDRE

I wanted to cry when Derrick and I ran into Ms. Ann. I had avoided men and him since moving to Miami but when I got a four day assignment in St. Augustine I called him and invited him down. There had been no contact so I wasn't sure he would come. Since moving, Maynard and I had sex very infrequently and it was no better. I still hadn't mentioned counseling again. We had just had a tenth anniversary and that seemed anticlimactic. My life seemed perfect except for that. I told myself I could live without it but that Thursday evening when Derrick showed up at my hotel I invited him in...

It was Friday afternoon after another session in bed with Derrick I saw her. It was like facing all my sins standing in my face. Her eyes peered into my soul, I felt. I thought how ironic she would be there, then. I never felt more ashamed in my life though her face showed love and disappointment. After she walked away I no longer wanted lunch. Derrick was already planning to drive back to Jacksonville after lunch but was cool when I said I was no longer hungry. After he drove away, I tried calling Ms. Ann but she didn't answer. My heart ached but she once told me even loving mentors sometimes needed space. I had to give her that. I called Maynard.

"Hello Babe." Maynard answered.

"Hey. I got things wrapped up today. I'm going to fly home tonight."

"That's cool. Let me know when your flight gets in." He sounded happy about my early return. I hadn't even needed to come down, I could see the items online and I knew the vendors but I wanted to get away and here I was.

"See you soon."

"I love you Audre."

"Me too." I said before disconnecting.

BASED ON MY EXPERIENCES
Daria's Reasons

"Girl, how can you be so pro black but not date Black men?" Daria's friend and assistant, Menia asked. Daria was twenty-four and in her final year of graduate school... and on the front lines for justice for Black people. She fought for equal health care, schooling, jobs and earnings and against police brutality but refused to date Black men. In the five years she dated, she never had. Any dating she did was hidden because of that.

"One thing has nothing to do with the other Menia. I prefer non-black men the same way you prefer tall men, its preference." Menia's eyes flickered over Daria, a dark skinned, tall, lean, shapely woman. It was hard to call her beautiful but more than anything she was stunning. Her skin was ebony, her hair almost nonexistent but dark blonde and her features exaggerated with very slanted eyes, large bow lips, flared nostrils and angled cheek bones. Those features with her lean body made her look like a model. Her nickname was Eagle.

"Umm hmm. I don't buy it. I see all the shade you give brothers. I'm sure they think you're lesbian."

A frown flickered over Daria's face.

"Perhaps that's a reason right there. Brothers always seem to feel if you won't screw them... specifically, you must be lesbian. I'm not; I just have no time to struggle for the cause and struggle in my relationship. All I see is y'all and your *struggle love*. No thanks."

Menia didn't argue with that. She had her share of failed relationships with Black men but for her there were no other. The love might be struggle but they struggled together. To date the Aryan looking men she saw Daria with was unthinkable.

Daria had her reasons but shared them exclusively with her mentor, confidante. Her grandmother, Louise referred her to the woman when she was fifteen; a year after her mother was killed by her father.

NINE YEARS EARLIER

"Come in and have a seat, I'm Ann Mitchell. "The tall woman said and stood until Daria was seated. Daria was fifteen and months earlier her mom was buried after being killed by her dad. Their relationship was always volatile. Dorothea and William had bonded over drugs, alcohol and nightlife. Daria spent most of her time with her grandmother but adored her beautiful mother and loved her charming father but they weren't good together. She recalled the night the police came to tell Louise; William had choked Dorothea until she stopped breathing. She was at the morgue and William arrested. Louise had walked through the home crying and raging about no good black men and how they ruined women. That was her mantra for weeks in between burying her daughter and officially adopting Daria. Of all the things Daria remembered it was those words. Louise advised her against men, especially Black ones who in her words used women up and either dumped or killed them. Dorothea, according to Louise lost everything once she gave herself to William and had his child. Prior to that she traveled the world as a stewardess. Daria was born when she was thirty two and Dorothea gave up flying to be with William, a professional gambler and nightclub manager.

"What do you want to share with me Daria?"
Daria pushed her glasses up on her nose and
stared at the woman, thinking she sounded like a
man.

"Nothing. My grandma made me come."

"Okay." Ann said and picked up her newspaper
and started reading. Daria stared at her surprised
she wasn't making her talk. She was there because
since her mom died, she had less to say and she
was never a big talker. It was hard enough going
to school with kids who knew her mom was killed
by her dad and her dad was in prison. The past
three months had been better because she was now
in a private school but not by much. There she
stood out as the only black girl student.

"I guess I need to talk about my mom dying."
Daria said fifteen minutes later. And folded her
newspaper, placing it on the table.

"What about it?"

"That I miss her, it's not fair and it's hard being
me right now."

"How is it hard being you, Daria?"

"In my neighborhood the boys call me Tar Baby or
Black Baby. The girls call me skinny black bitch

and stuff. They always did but now they talk about my mom and dad. At my school they don't know that stuff but I'm the only black girl. There are about ten black boys but they are all jocks and date White girls. They ignore me which is fine. I just want to go to college and get away from here. It's hell."

Ann felt the softly spoken words deep inside. She knew it had to be hell to have lost her father and mother the way she did and deal with the meanness of high school peers or their indifference.

"You do know you're beautiful and brilliant and kids Black nor white know how to deal with that. You're also very self-possessed and mature. Most fifteen year olds aren't."

"That's because most don't have real shit to deal with." Ann chuckled from deep in her throat for several minutes. That made Daria smile. She hadn't heard genuine laughter in a long time.

"That my dear is true shit. What interests you?" Daria pulled off her glasses and was more arresting. Ann realized the girl hid behind her faux glasses.

"I'm interested in justice. My grandma lives right on the edge of the hood and there are injustices in

*housing, policing and how food is distributed."
Ann sat up straight. The child knew her
community. Also my father would have gotten a
much longer sentence if justice for Black women
were a real thing. Especially at the hands of Black
men. He got five years for murdering the mother of
his only child."*

*Ann flinched because she had followed the story
and agreed but William Means had never been in
trouble with the law and took a deal.*

"So criminal justice as a major?"

*"No ma'am. I'll take it as a minor, math will be
my major. You're pretty easy to talk to. How do
you know my grandma?" Ann was in her mid-
fifties and Louise her late seventies.*

*"Ms. Louise knew my mom. My mom was beaten
by my stepfather; she was a conversation in the
hood." Daria's eyes widened. "There were many
black eyes, broken bones and busted lips from the
time I was ten to eighteen. It seemed to stop after I
went to college. They stayed married and died four
months apart." Daria was surprised because
nothing about Ann indicated that. She was also
stunned by the honesty. Most adults pretended
their lives were perfect. For instance she knew her
grandma was once a bootlegger in her twenties
through forties but would Louise would never*

admit it. Dorothea told Daria many stories from the past before Daria was born.

"How did you deal with it ma'am?"

"I had my Godma, books and school. No one really teased me about it. All our parents had issues during those days. We were there for each other. I was teased about being tall, stuck up and bookish but no name calling such as you endured. Also, my mom lived until I was in my mid-forties, she advocated for me against most people. My stepfather was the exception."

"Thanks for your honesty. Can I go; I'll come back in two days,"

"Of course."

Daria had been meeting with Ann for the nine years since. When she was an hour away at the University of Florida she had driven down for weekly sessions.

SCENE TWO

After leaving the jail Daria was tired. She spent the day trying to get them to provide more than two sanitary napkins per month to women in jail. When those ran out they used toilet paper or rags. It made Daria sick to think of it. More than anything she wanted food and wine. She was meeting with Ms. Ann for dinner but first going home to shower and changed. She lived in Louise's house. Louise died three years earlier at eighty three, leaving her the house and a hefty insurance policy. Daria worked as a college tutor and for her non-profit, *About Justice*. William had been released from prison four years earlier but left the state without contacting her. In nine years the hood was different, the homes were being purchased by yuppies and even better, young black couples with children. At four pm, people were walking dogs, pushing strollers and arriving home from work.

"What's up Daria?" Jerry Ramon said as she got her mail. Jerry lived across the street in his parents' home and had been one of her tormentors as a kid. In all fairness he never said anything but he was with her tormentors. Jerry was two years older and bought and refurbished homes. His was one of the nicest on the block. He was eye candy, tall, muscular, dark skinned with a soft beard and a ready smile. He was also close to Ms. Ann. Trying not to frown she turned to face him.

"I'm well Jerry. How are you?" She said in clipped tones. He had the audacity to laugh, showing a dimple and beautiful teeth.

"Daria, you're entirely too beautiful to be so mean. Enjoy your evening." He said, walking up his sidewalk. She grabbed her mail and walked slowly inside purposely. She heard what sounded like sardonic laughter. On paper Jerry was a great guy, he was educated, no kids or jail time and had bought his parents a new home on the Southside with profits from his business flipping houses and anyone with eyes could see his sex appeal but hell no. Besides she had Scotty for sex and conversation. That was good enough.

~~YYYYY~~

"You look cute." Ms. Ann said. Daria smirked. She was usually in jeans and a T-shirt or sweat shirt but tonight she was in a dress with sandals and African jewelry. Ms. Ann always wore dresses, usually black, skimming her curves even in her sixties. That evening was no exception.

"Trying to be like you ma'am." Daria had always called her ma'am and was one of her favorite protégés except for the Black man thing. They rarely discussed it. Though Ann remembered their first conversation about it. Daria was nineteen and just lost her virginity to Brad, a white college friend. Daria came to her crying.

"Ms. Ann he seemed obsessed with my skin color and he said he thought I would smell differently. Smell like what?"

Ann held her close, allowing her to cry until spent before responding.

"Baby, there are so many myths out there. We are different and he's young and uninformed. Did he hurt you?"

"No, he pleased me with oral sex which he seemed obsessed with after deciding I smelled good. The intercourse was painful initially but mediocre. It just felt embarrassing."

"You should never feel embarrassed in bed with a man. That's why I love Black men and they have loved me." Daria pulled back at those words.

"A Black man killed my mom." Ann was never able to counteract that and Brad didn't stop her from taking other lovers. Scotty her current lover was good but it was purely sexual and no real connection.

"How was the meeting today?" Ann asked.

"Okay. I'm just horrified that we are having to beg for freaking sanitary napkins as if we are a third world country. It's horrendous."

"I agree. But I'm so proud of you. You're making a difference in the city."

"Again like you. Ms. Ann, you're an icon. We all love you because you're in the trenches and you don't have to be. I saw Jerry today." Ann beamed. She loved Jerry, he was an asset to his community, refurbishing homes and mentoring young men.

"How is he?"

"Annoying." Daria said.

"That's my boy you're talking about. He's so many good things. Next Friday we are having a block party to celebrate Black folks who support and live in the community. Jerry is being honored. Its two blocks from you. You should come; there will be food and local talent. Jerry deserves all of this." Daria wrinkled her nose feeling a bit jealous. Ms. Ann had become her surrogate mother over the past nine years. She was often jealous of her other young'uns as she called them. And there were many.

"I might make an appearance since its close by. Is Mr. Mitchell coming?"

"Of course. He does not trust me around all those fine young men." Daria rolled her eyes but knew it was true. The young men who knew Ms. Ann loved and would kill for her.

~~YYYYY~~

"Am I your secret white man Daria?" Scotty asked after sex. She called him and stopped by after dinner with Ms. Ann. He had never been to her place. They had been out together but never as people who were involved, always with others. Daria rolled off the bed and pulled on her underwear. She hated the conversation, it was the same one she had with the previous two guys she saw. After getting dressed she sat on a bench at the foot of his bed.

"Scotty, we are friends... friends with good benefits. I have no secrets." He sat up in bed the sheets draping over the lower half of his body. It always startled Daria how white he was with ash brown hair and light grey eyes. He was handsome and well built by any estimation and was a civil rights attorney six years older than her. He provided great pro bono services for her clients.

"Daria, you are filled with secrets. I'm just not interested in being one of them. I like you... a lot and I want to date you, take you out. I'm beyond the sex every couple of weeks when you're horny, angry or sad." Daria's skin prickled at his words. They were true but she didn't like hearing them. She liked and respected Scotty but wasn't remotely interested in what he offered. She knew it was time to move on.

"I'm sorry you feel that way. I like you Scotty, a lot but I'm twenty four with ambitions that don't include dating... or anything serious." She said, grabbing her oversized leather bag.

"My legal services will always be available to you." Scotty said coolly. Daria nodded as she made her way from the room and out the house. She made sure to lock his door. She realized she felt nothing. Beyond her mom, grandma, Ms. Ann and her causes she hadn't invested in feelings since she was a child.

Jerry and a few friends were in his yard when Daria drove up. She tried to ignore them but Jerry yelled out to her, "Sleep well Aria." She expected laughter from the other guys but it didn't occur. They were all looking at the beautiful woman who lived across from Jerry.

"Jerry, you have the best view from here." One said. Jerry smiled but said nothing. He completely agreed.

SCENE TWO

Daria got dressed for the block party but was wavering. She attended many because they were often funding her interests but most were a nice mix of people. She knew this one would be mostly Black people and if she were to go to confession she would have to admit that other than her clients and a handful of others she didn't have much interaction with her own people. She convinced herself since she sought justice and resources for mostly Black people that covered her but she suspected only she agreed with her own justifications. She was a great dancer thanks to her mom and years of dance and loved music but in college she was either alone or in very diverse groups of people socially.

As she decided not to go, Ms. Ann and Mr. Mitchell pulled up to her gate. She could only grin and grab her bag. She was dressed in black tights with a long, snug purple mini dress with the word #Justice in black letters on the front. Her feet were encased in black ballet shoes with strong soles.

"Hello Mr. Mitchell, I thank you for driving here of your own accord." Daria said once she was in the backseat. Ms. Ann threw her a look.

"Young lady, I'm just the chauffeur." He said.

The first person they saw upon arrival was Jerry, dressed in all black, his handsome face, smiling as he shook Mr. Mitchell's hand after embracing Ms. Ann.

"Thank you Daria for attending our little event." He said his eyes boring into her. It was hardly little; there were food trucks donating food and a huge stage with musicians. There was also a good bit of diversity but mostly Black and brown people.

"My pleasure." Daria offered, looking around.

Mr. Magic, a ten minute song by Grover Washington started. Jerry grabbed Ms. Ann's hand and they danced down to the stage. Mr. Mitchell said, "We better join in." Daria followed him with reluctance but soon became engaged in the groove. They played four songs in quick succession and she danced with Mr. Mitchell for all the songs but they had nothing on Jerry and Ms. Ann, they were serious dancers and it was clear they danced together many times before. They seemed to enjoy the reggae songs most. There was a lull for people to get food and drinks and Daria was grateful. She hadn't given into to dance like that in a long time. Before she could reach a food truck, Jerry walked up, handing her a bottle of frosty water. She took it, thanking him.

"You're welcome. Come sit with me." He said, leading her to a table for two. Clearly he was used to being followed because he didn't look back. She glanced around for The Mitchells. They were standing in line at the French fry truck. When she arrived at the table, Jerry was standing, holding out a chair. She sat down and drank down her water. He sat across from her.

"You're an amazing dancer Daria." Jerry said, staring at her.

"Lots of lessons and my mom was a great dancer." She almost bit her tongue. Jerry remembered her mother.

"She was very beautiful also." Dorothea had been beautiful with slightly lighter skin than Daria and long, curly hair. Men said she was beautiful to be so dark. Daria needed to change the subject.

"You and Ms. Ann dance well together. Mr. Mitchell was watching y'all." A broad smile covered Jerry's face, his teeth shining in the darkness.

"He should. He knows I'm in love with his wife, me and many others. You're close to them aren't you?"

"Mr. Mitchell is here for her, he tolerates us because she loves us." Daria said. Jerry nodded in agreement. "But Ms. Ann is my family, my matriarch."

Jerry could hear the love in her voice.

"That's great. I'm glad you're here Daria. This is your community as well. You're doing great work for us and we appreciate you." She fastened her eyes on him.

"Do y'all. Or am I just the bougie, dark skin girl out of touch with the hood?" Jerry blinked, looking surprised by what she said.

"If that's what you think, you *are* out of touch. We admire you and you've always been part of this hood. We know you could leave and do so much else but you're right here among us. Honestly, I thought you would leave."

"Why?" She asked, surprised she really wanted to know. She stretched her long legs out. Jerry glanced at them quickly before refocusing on the conversation.

"Because of how mean kids were to you growing up, especially after you lost your mama. I didn't say anything but I was with them. The truth is I was intimidated by how beautiful you were and sophisticated after all you went through. I regretted many days never defending you. But look at you Daria, you're doing big things and many of those kids are on the block or struggling to hold it together. But here you are." He said earnestly.

"Here we are. After you got hurt in college you came back here and you could leave anytime. I know how many places you've refurbished outside the hood."

"You been checking on me?" He asked.

"I don't have to; Ms. Ann handles your PR quite well. She's very proud of you."

"She's proud of us Daria. All of us who handle our business but I'm here because this is my home."

"I'm here for the same reason Jerry. I'm going to The Fish truck, I'm starving,"

"Enjoy." He said. He wanted to talk more but he was patient. He was also hosting a party. He watched her strut across the street before tossing away their bottles and going back to his guests. After getting her food, she joined The Mitchells.

"This is great." Ms. Ann said, peering at her. She had watched Daria and Jerry interact. Mr. Mitchell told her to mind *her* business.

"It tis." Daria responded noncommittally before stuffing her mouth with spicy, fried shrimp. Mr. Mitchell chuckled, watching his wife. Daria was on to Ann.

Daria danced with several other people throughout the evening but only saw Jerry in passing. She tried convincing herself she didn't notice he never asked her to dance.

On the way out he said close to her ear, "We *will* converse more and soon. See you on our block."

SCENE THREE

"Daria, I know you're busy but Scotty ghosted our client twice." Menia said. Daria glanced up, annoyance on her face. It had been three weeks since she saw Scotty but he assured her he would come through.

"Twice?"

"Yes, one time isn't a big deal but twice is. I called Magnum Augustine. There is a fee associated but he needed representation."

"You did the right thing. Scratch Scotty off and I'll find another pro bono attorney." Menia stood in the doorway, her face scrunched up in thought.

"The hood is full of young up and coming attorneys dying to work with us."

"I'm sure they're not dying Menia but get me a list. I have never recruited the attorneys who worked for us by the way, they volunteered." There was aggravation in Daria's tone but Menia smiled. They were friends and truth telling was part of it.

"Yes, Scotty volunteered because he wanted you... now for reasons unbeknownst to me, he has unvolunteered. I'll get that list." Menia strolled away before Daria could respond. Daria sucked her teeth but picked up the phone and dialed Ms. Ann, telling her, the dilemma.

"Sweetie, I can't think of anyone offhand but Jerry has a roster of attorneys he works with who handles pro bono cases. I'm sure he could assist you."

Daria hadn't seen Jerry since the block party two weeks earlier. Lately when she returned home his truck was gone. It was late spring and the weather was great so he was likely very busy. It seemed Jerry was connected to the vein of everything in the community.

"If you would give him my number..."

"I would be delighted to."

Daria hung up and gathered her things. She had two students to tutor and a late meeting.
~~YYYYY~~

Jerry was getting out of his truck when Daria pulled up to her mailbox. He walked across the street to talk to her. She rolled down her window to give him access.

"Hello Daria, Ms. Ann gave me your number. I need to shower and change but I have what you need." A shock of desire pierced her at his words and the scent of man and mint that wafted from him. "Come over in about an hour and a half, I'll order food."

"Okay." Was all Daria could manage. She needed a shower herself. She watched him walk across the road and go inside.

Daria arrived exactly an hour and a half later. She had showered and changed her hair color from dark blonde to deep auburn. She loved temporary hair wax colors. She was wearing a cotton maxi dress the same color as her hair. Her skin was shiny with care and moisturizer.

"Damn." Jerry said when he opened the door. "You're gorgeous woman."

"Can I come in?" Daria asked. He moved, allowing her inside. The scent of lime and coconut assaulted his senses. He had to take several deep breaths because he knew his arousal was showing in his loose sweats. He turned around to find her checking out the art on his wall. It was mostly of ocean scenes but there were a few Black people interspersed in them.

"These are dope. Who is the artist?" Daria asked.

"Jerry Ramon." He said. She reacted by swiveling to face him.

"Wow. These are great. In fact your home is nice." The huge living room was mostly low leather furniture in shades of brown, bookshelves and tables. The long windows were covered with open, taupe blinds and the floor was the original hardwood from the sixties when the home was built.

"Thank you. I work hard and painting keeps me chill. So does reading, I love accurate history. Follow me to the kitchen I cooked shrimp, I saw you chowing down at the block party. These aren't fried but sautéed in garlic oil and pepper flakes. There is bread, salad and beer." She followed him, trying not to look at his hard ass under his sweats. He slid a Tecate brew as she sat at his island. His kitchen was strictly utilitarian and full of sunlight with a patio door overlooking his backyard. She watched him fill plates with chunks of bread and the shrimp. She was surprised when he prayed over the food. Her grandma and Ms. Ann were the only people in her life who did that.

"This is so good." Daria said after several bites. She loved shrimp. Jerry grinned at her placing a chunk of sauce dipped bread in his mouth. The sauce was garlicky and spicy.

"I love to cook. My mom taught me early to cook, clean and do laundry. I was an only child but I had hella chores. Did you?"

"Of course, Louise made me work but school was her main thing."

After eating two servings, Jerry gave Daria a list of four attorneys.

"These brothers are all good and will work with and for you and your people. Utilize them." Daria's eyes filled. She had never had such options. Jerry watched her and wanted to touch her but didn't dare.

"Thank you. This is a lot. It will make a huge difference."

"Daria, I'm at your disposal, just ask. These brothers are all married by the way."

She looked up in puzzlement.

"Huh?"

"I don't want them trying to date you."

"Why do you care?"

"Because I want to date you. I've wanted to date you since we were in high school but..."

"You heard I didn't date in high school and then that I don't date brothers."

"Were they lying?"

"I've never really dated period. I've hung out with a few guys but this what we are doing... not that this is a date or anything, I've not done that. And no, no brothers." She met his eyes defiantly.

"Why Daria?"

"The first brother I loved killed my Mama." Jerry felt her pain deep in his gut. He understood that. "Before killing her, he demeaned her in front of me, saying she was too black, her ass and lips were too big but claimed to love her. I look like her and am even darker. My grandma tried to explain it was his way of keeping her small and his. I wanted no part of that and all through high school the brothers tormented me about my skin, lips, eyes and ass. Why would I Jerry?"

"I'm so sorry that was your life Daria. I also understand why you would feel that way but don't judge all of us by that. Don't judge me by that. You're so beautiful, smart and loving. Your love is just all about your work. You need that love to be bigger than that."

Jerry stood and pulled her into his arms, holding her until her body relaxed into his. After several minutes he covered her mouth with his and she melted into his mouth. He kissed her more thoroughly than she had ever been kissed and more thoroughly than he had ever kissed anyone. When he took her hand, leading her to his bedroom, she followed, allowing him to undress her, place her on his bed. He made love slowly to her entire body. He savored her, loving her into opening up her body and spirit to him, allowing him fully inside. By the time he covered himself and entered her, his name was pouring from her throat as tears raced down her cheeks. Tears he licked away. She had never been touched so deeply or fully.

"I'm not going to allow you to run away from me Daria." Jerry said, looking down at her. She swallowed deeply because she wanted to stay forever but she also wanted to flee. It was if he had peeled away her armor in two hours; the armor that protected her fragile heart.

"Okay... but I really need to pee and drink something."

"You go pee and I'll get water."

After peeing, she stared at herself in the mirror.
She looked like herself but no longer felt like her.
She was going to have to get used to that because
she could admit she wanted more of Jerry and
might even need more. She returned to him back in
bed, still naked with glasses of water. She walked
slowly to him in all her glory, climbing back in
bed with him. She drank her water before placing
her head on his chest.

"I've not seen my dad since..."

"Do you want to see him?"

"Not yet but I feel one day I might have to if for no
other reason than to fully close that door."

"Daria, cross that bridge then, now just live, do
your work and learn to love... and be loved."

~~YYYYY~~

Several months later Daria and Jerry are growing
their relationship. She's in no way ready to see
William but knows she might have to one day but
living, working and loving is healing her...

I LOVE HIM, BUT...
Phaedra's Justifications

Phaedra loved Carlton and their daughter, Carla. They were married ten years and were successful together and apart. Phaedra owned a successful gift shop selling body and hair oils and worked with Carlton in his very successful detailing business. Carlton also prepared meat for several local catering companies and events. His steaks, ribs and chops were legendary. They had a nice home and looked great together. They were both tall and athletic, having played high school and college ball. Phaedra had massive natural curls and Carlton shoulder length dreads. Everything about them screamed Black Love and success but Phaedra had been sexually involved with her best friend, Anisha since college. She had great, regular sex with Carlton but enjoyed Anisha's touch as well. It had worked well for years but Anisha was tired at thirty-five and wanted a full time lover. Phaedra had to find a way to let go.

SCENE ONE

The first time Phaedra saw Carlton she was enamored. She was twenty- three, with a brand new business and car and was an accountant at Victoria's Secret. She walked into *Carl's Car Spot* and was greeted by Carl. He was six feet-four inches to her five eleven and handsome with medium brown skin, tats, baby dreads, muscles and a beautiful smile. His greeting sealed her attraction.

"Damn, it's Phaedra from the U. My favorite female baller. How you doing baby?" He said in his southern drawl.

"I'm good Carl from Florida State, I see you." Carlton was two years older and had turned his dad's mechanic shop into the detailing spot after graduating from college. For both of them college and sports had been the means to an education not professional balling.

"Nah baby, I see you." Phaedra was dressed in snug sweat shorts and a cropped top, showing off her honed curves. Carlton loved curvy women with a bit of musculature and Phaedra was all that. "I'm going to personally hook up that Accord and then take your fine ass to dinner."

"I eat a lot."

"Me too baby, me too." He said that and licked his full bottom lip. Heat shot through Phaedra.

After her car was spotless, Phaedra followed Carlton to a barbecue joint on the north side. They ate a rack of ribs, wings and drank Heineken until the place closed. Afterwards he followed her home, promising to eat dessert another time. After that they were almost inseparable. He proved his abilities and she reveled in his attention. The one problem was Anisha. She didn't understand how Phaedra could have a relationship with Carlton that included sex and still make love to her. A year later when Carlton and Phaedra got married Anisha disappeared for two years but returned in time to become godmother to Carla. It took another year before they became sexual again.

~~¥¥¥¥¥¥~~

"I have to go for me Phaedra. I want what you have with Carlton but with a woman." Anisha said. Phaedra stopped working on the accounts and faced her.

"Then have it. No one has ever stood in the way of your relationships Anisha. Certainly not me."

"You have though; I only love you. I want to be faithful to one person and not being with someone but being available to you. That's been my life Phaedra. I need to leave to do this. We aren't even partners in this business. I work here, you own all of it."

"Do you need to own some of it Anisha? Will that make this stop?" Phaedra's voice was filled with aggravation.

"No. I am thirty five; I need an identity apart from you. In college we were just fooling around. Or that's what I convinced myself but I wasn't. I was in love. You married Carlton and I dipped but came back. That worked but now it doesn't. I'm a lesbian Phaedra. I'm not bisexual like you or just freaky like some. I want a committed relationship. You can't give me that, you're committed to Carlton and Carla."

"I'm as committed as I can be. I spend more time with you than anyone."

"But you live with him, dream with him and will never leave him. I want and need that with someone and you're not it." Anisha said before leaving the office. Phaedra agreed with her on everything. Carlton was aware of and unbothered by her and Anisha as long as it didn't affect them. He told her that years ago after she confessed the affair after Anisha left.

"Anisha and I became intimate in college. We were friends and roommates who were sexual." Phaedra confessed.

"Aren't many women freaking in college a little bit, especially ballers? I've heard lots of stories..."

"It's a thing but I'm not sure about many. I think Anisha is more than just freaking though."

"Anisha ain't my problem. As long as you weren't doing more than freaking I'm cool. Now if Anisha were a man we would have problems." When Anisha returned and came to work with Phaedra they didn't discuss it again, she was family. Carlton treated Anisha like a sister.

"I need to see Ms. Ann." Phaedra said to the empty room.

~~YYYYY~~

"She deserves that Phaedra. The same as you have your life." Ms. Ann said. Phaedra knew she would but it still stung. "You can always leave Carlton and be with her."

"That's not happening."

"Then let her go."

"She's my friend. I can give up the... intimacy, that's rare nowadays anyway but she's my best friend... after Carlton."

"That's the problem Sweetie. She feels she was before Carlton but once you met him she was after..."

Shocked clarity filled Phaedra. She rarely discussed Anisha with Ms. Ann but the truth was finally spilled. Anisha had been first from age eighteen until twenty three and Phaedra walked in that shop. After that it was Carlton, Carla and then Anisha.

"More importantly whoever she finds will not be like Carlton. He knows you're devoted to him, to your family. Her new partner, when there's one will likely not be that understanding. Let her go Phaedra. You will have to say to her, she's free to go. It's much like when a family member is dying, they often hold on until we free them in words and deeds."

"Dang Ms. Ann, you are a sage. I hate that you're right but you are. I don't like losing Anisha but losing Carlton would kill me."

"Exactly. Let *her* live."

~~YYYYY~~

Phaedra went to Anisha's before going home. Anisha opened the door and looked startled.

"Nisha, who is that?" A feminine voice called out. Within seconds, Sienna Mayweather, one the business' customers walked up behind Anisha. Sienna was a hairstylist who used the products. Phaedra backed up a bit.

"My bad. I was just stopping by to agree to the terms you set forth earlier Anisha. Though you aren't an owner by definition, your severance package will be more than fair." Phaedra said. A range of emotions flickered across Anisha's face. Sienna simply looked smug. "Stop by at your convenience to sign the paperwork." Phaedra said before walking to her truck, her heart aching in her chest. It was time to fully discuss with Carlton. She felt Anisha discussed them with Sienna.

~~YYYYY~~

Carla was in her room when Phaedra arrived home. She checked on her before going to the kitchen where Carlton had an array of spices all over the counter. He personally ground the spices he used for his steak, briskets and ribs. It was Thursday and he cooked all night and Friday morning to meet the needs of his extensive client lists. His brothers worked for him running the detail store on Friday's and Saturday's. He loved both worlds but cooking meat edged out detailing. When he cooked, he always wore a white chef coat. Carlton glanced up when Phaedra dropped into a chair at the table.

"You look like you lost your best friend. What's up?"

"I think I did. Anisha is moving on."

"What this time?" Carlton asked, placing his grinder on the counter and cleaning his hands.

"The same. You know Anisha and I still..."

"Hooked up sexually... Yea I figured as much. It hasn't affected me yet or has it?" Phaedra met his eyes. He watched her as he meticulously seasoned the meat covering the table.

"Hell no. Nothing affects us. Carl, more than anything Anisha is my friend. When I got to

Miami we became fast friends. She was upper middle class and I was from the hood, a girl raised by her dad and older brothers, all ballers. She and I were different than the others and that was our bond. The sex, at least to me was secondary to the bond. Anisha is the only woman I've been with. But it seems I've been a selfish bitch for holding on to her. When she returned I should have left it strictly friends. I held on to her and I had you... that's just wrong. I am giving her severance and letting it go."

"I know it's hard but Phaedra this is it. There will be no other person replacing her." Carlton said and Phaedra looked up, stricken by what he said.

"Of course not, why would you even say that?"

"Because I dealt with this because I felt woman sex is something you needed. By the time I knew I was in love and decided to live with it to keep you. But if it's done with Anisha, it's done."

"It's done. I can't explain it to you but it's done. I've not sought out Anisha for sex in years but admit when she sought me out..."

"I get it Phaedra or I wouldn't be here, I'm just putting it all on the table."

"Carlton, I choose you. I get that it doesn't look like that..."

"Then it's done. I need to get this meat seasoned and in the smoker. I have three restaurants and two events to cook for." Phaedra nodded in understanding. Carlton had a huge smoker on their property.

"Can I help?"

"Get payroll ready for the shop for tomorrow. I'm not going to get to it."

"I got it. Thanks Carlton." He nodded and went to get the meat out the walk-in freezer. Phaedra went to her office. They had businesses to run.

~~YYYYY~~

Phaedra felt Carlton come up behind her, the scent of meat smoke permeating the air. She had dozed off after completing payroll, getting dinner for Carla and putting her to bed. No one bothered Carlton when he was outside cooking. He always had old school music and his meat. He didn't even take his phone outside with him. She opened her eyes and he placed a tray table in front of her with medium rare steak and chopped salad. There were even wet wipes for her face and hands with a glass

of wine. He had showered and changed into old
SFU sweats.

"What time is it?" She asked.

"Midnight. I've been out there six hours.
Everything is good. I know you fed Carla but
didn't eat." She made a face as she washed up. He
knew her so well.

"I was hoping for this. Did you eat?"

"I did. The food should be ready by six am. How
long you been sleep?"

"About three hours." Phaedra cut into her steak
and moaned as the flavors exploded on her tongue.
"So good."

Carlton nodded in appreciation. He knew his food
was fire but loved hearing it, especially from his
wife.

"Carl, why did you tolerate me with Anisha?"

"I felt it was a package deal honestly. Also, I'm
not threatened by her. I know what we have
together. She was a known entity. I was also a
young nigga when we met, I had done some dirt by
then and as you know I wasn't fully committed
until we had Carla. I expect no more from you than

from myself. I also knew once she returned it was a now and then thing. It was just our life." He said, leaning back in his lounger. He would sleep about three hours and then get up to check on his food. This was their Friday nights.

"Phaedra, you're my wife. Period."

"I am. I love you."

"I love you, now eat and let me close my eyes a few."

Carlton woke up at four and Phaedra was asleep in her recliner. He covered her and went outside for a couple more hours. He kissed her softly before going.

SCENE TWO

The office was quiet when Phaedra arrived Monday but Anisha was waiting inside.

"Phaedra, I could work a bit longer if you need me." Anisha offered.

"Anisha, that won't be necessary. It's time, past time for this. I've held on long enough, keeping you from living fully. I made the mistake of getting friendship and... Sexual intimacy mixed up. I own it. Are you staying in Jacksonville?" Anisha looked as if she were going to cry. She was very emotional, always had been. In college Phaedra felt Anisha made her give in to softness whereas she provided strength for Anisha. That was their relationship wrapped up.

"I have to give a months' notice but then I'm moving to Orlando. Sienna is opening a new shop there." Phaedra wasn't going to address Sienna. But she was going to let her know she spoke to Carlton.

"I told Carlton what was what. It's time for me to focus on my main life before I no longer have it. I wish you only the best, you've been the best friend I've had Anisha, bar none."

Phaedra took a seat to take her checkbook from the desk. Anisha held up her hand.

"I can't allow you to do that. You don't have to pay me; I added nothing to your business."

"You don't have a choice Anisha. You were here when Carlton was selling my stuff out the shop to keep the lights on in this building. Also, this has to be a clean cut, no going back." Phaedra filled out the check and printed out the release form she printed the night before.

Anisha's eyes widened at the check amount. Tears filled her eyes when she read the finality and professionalism of the form. It ended all professional ties, indicating though Anisha Powers had no investment in the business she was being compensated for her invaluable dedication to the business. Anisha quickly signed and stood by as Phaedra called in her notary friend to notarize and provide them copies.

"Phaedra, I had to do this." Anisha said, her voice shaking.

"I know and I agree. I was selfish with your love." Phaedra stood, embracing her friend before letting go.

Phaedra dropped into her chair, taking a deep
breath. She had work to do.

"Are you okay?" Ms. Ann asked two weeks after
Anisha left.

"Yes ma'am. It's been hard admitting I was so
selfish. I maintained sexual intimacy with my best
friend to keep her close while having Carlton who
has proven what love truly is. That is chasing me."

"You must learn to let it go. Anisha provided many
things you didn't have. Your mom left when you
were tiny and you were raised by men, big
masculine men. You were family to a girl with a
family but felt like an orphan."

Phaedra had to grin. Her dad had gotten Ms. Ann
to mentor his little dudette when Phaedra was in
sixth grade. He felt she needed softening up. That
didn't occur but she grew to adore time with the
woman who made her read books and talk about
her feelings.

Meeting her roommate Anisha, she found in her a
very feminine woman with a fragile spirit. She was
raised by two very successful parents who were
ambitious for her rather than allowing her to
choose. Anisha ended up a teacher not the attorney

her parents wanted. They didn't disinherit her but she felt cast out from them. They hadn't talked to her in years in anything more than perfunctory ways and to send money she never spent.

"True. I'm grateful for you Ms. Ann and my husband."

"That man of yours is as you say, the real MVP."

"That's a word."

Anisha's Take

I fell hard for Phaedra the day she showed up as my roommate. She seemed so sure and confident with swagger. She had a huge curly Afro, perfect skin, and a girly face though her demeanor was butch in the way lots of girl ballers are whether they are lesbians are not. Her attire was form-fitting Nike wear showing off her perfect body. She looked like I would if I were confident enough. At twelve I knew I preferred girls but I had to hide it from Mike and Ellen Powers. They were attorneys raising attorneys and I didn't want to be that but to teach school. To admit I was also a lesbian would have been too much. I didn't talk to my parents they talked to me. But with Phaedra we had conversations. I remember the first night; she was lying on her bed in tight shorts and a sports bra.

"I love finance so I'm majoring in business. I'm not interested in the WNBA though my dad would love that but more than anything he wanted me educated. My oldest brother is in the NBA and my next oldest is playing in Japan. Dad raised me just like them." Anisha listened fascinated.

"And your mom?" Anisha saw Phaedra's face still.

"She left when I was four. They got pregnant with my brother when mom was a senior in high school and dad a sophomore in college. He quit college to work to provide for and raise us. He was devoted to his kids but when my brothers were ten, seven and I was four, mom decided she wanted to live and dad let her go. Now dad lives very well thanks to Avery. He bought dad a nice home and truck when he signed his contract, way out the hood. But dad still works. He says he's going to get his pension though he's only forty eight he can retire in ten years."

"He sounds like a great guy."

"He's the best. What about your people?"

"Mike and Ellen are both third generation attorneys and wanted the same for me but I always wanted to teach elementary education. I'm a huge disappointment to them in many ways. We talk once a month and they send checks mostly from money my maternal grandmother left me through mom until I'm thirty.

Within the first week I told Phaedra I was lesbian and she wasn't fazed. She knew many lesbians. She didn't confess any sexual preference. Men and women fawned over her. Our first sexual encounter was initiated by me. One night after a big argument with my mom, I got in bed with

Phaedra and she consoled me while I cried. I kissed her and she didn't resist and for months we were hot and heavy. She was a virgin and we were young and horny. She got involved with one of the male ballers and we tapered off but there were times I needed her comfort and she never rebuffed me. The same thing happened after she married Carlton. While they dated and got to know each other we weren't intimate. I was very jealous and had sex with lots of women but Phaedra was happy with her new love and life.

About a year after they married we went to a weekend conference together. She was growing her business and took me along. In the middle of the night, much as I had in college I got in bed with her and she provided the comfort only she could. I hoped she might decide I was her preference but she never did and never initiated sexual contact. I ran away but returned, willing to settle whatever she could offer. I loved, I love Phaedra, but Sienna convinced me I deserve more than Phaedra and what she offers. I'm going away this time because I need to convince myself its true. I'm convinced Phaedra is done this time and probably grateful now. That feels like a knife in my gut.

I DON'T LOVE HIM BUT
Chelsea's Truth

Chelsea Swift never loved her husband Robert, she didn't love him currently. She married him because for the third time in her life, she lost everything she had and needed someone to support her. They met at a club and danced together several times and he bought her drinks. She recalled him saying, "I love skinny women with red hair."

She had grinned, saying, "Only the hair on my head is red, the rest of it is dark brown. I'm usually partial to men who are bigger than you."

"Oh, I'm big enough." He responded cockily. Later that night, she discovered he was and was better than average at using his bigness but she was long past caring about sex. What Chelsea wanted was to be funded. He said during their conversation at the bar he earned seventeen hundred per week after taxes. At the time she was getting by on six hundred a week before taxes. That worked for her. But let's get some backstory.

SCENE ONE

At twenty nine Chelsea was working as a bartender in an upscale Detroit bar. She was Detroit born and bred but always wanted to leave but the opportunity never presented itself. She was known for dating professional football players but they never manifested. Two were relatively long term but ended in one marrying a close friend of hers and the other moving on after getting out of the league. She recalled the words the aunt who raised her spoke, *"Chelsea, you're too easy, you fall in with these guys, trade sex for a few gifts and they leave. They feel they done met your standards."* Chelsea had sucked her teeth and rolled her eyes not listening to the old woman.

Detron Baker strolled into *Drink Well* as if he owned the place. Everyone recognized his as the linebacker for the Jacksonville Panthers football team. He was tall, big, handsome and loud with a ready smile and witty quips. He was photogenic and easygoing, the media loved him. His team had rolled over the Detroit team earlier and he was in rare form.

"All the ladies can get drunk on Detron!" He yelled and the women all applauded and tried getting as close to him as possible. Chelsea watched him from behind the bar, feeling glad she had tightened up her hair and makeup before work. Chelsea was almond colored and thin with huge breasts. She found that with many men her breasts and skin color made her very attractive to them.

She also played up her light eyes with makeup. Some ignored her because she had a flat butt but she grew used to that in her teens. She was wearing tight white jeans and a black tunic that flared a bit over her behind with stacked heels for style and height but was comfortable. She watched Detron until he made his way to the bar, his smiling eyes taking her in. She noted he was young, younger than her. She would later learn he was twenty four.

"What's up Red? You're a cute lil thing. Whatchu got back there?" She could tell he was playing up the slang, beneath it she heard educated. Turning away from him she quickly mixed what she called Chelsea's Iced Tea which included four forms of alcohol, cola and lemon. After shaking it she poured it over ice and handed it to him. He took a hefty swig, his eyes never leaving hers as he climbed up on a stool at the bar. People, mostly women gathered around him. Chelsea didn't care; either Detron was interested in them or her. She didn't sweat other women like that. She did watch how he interacted with others and noted he was generous, funny and kind. She had seen many in his position demean people but there was none of that in Detron. He seemed to genuinely like people.

At the end of the night he asked if she wanted to hangout. He was surprisingly sober, he bought lots of drinks but only drank two and lots of water.

"Sure." She said. She followed him out and a driver took them to The Westin Book Cadillac Detroit Hotel. Detron told her he would be there three days. Chelsea spent those three days with him, mostly in his bed. Detron was good at sex without much finesse. He liked lots of hard sex and had extreme stamina. Chelsea was down for it and called out of work. The morning he prepared to leave he invited her to come with him.

"What would I do there?" She asked.

"Chill with me. We have similar appetites. I'll hook you up with clothes and shit. You don't have any kids do you?"

"No kids and no real family, other than my aunt. I board with her." Chelsea said, hopeful he was serious. She wanted nothing more than to get the hell out of Detroit. Her goal was before twenty five but before thirty would be just fine.

"Let's do it then." He said. That morning he bought her a Dior trunk for almost four thousand dollars and allowed her to fill it with designer clothes, shoes and underwear before they flew to Jacksonville.

Chelsea felt Detron was her ticket and for almost two years he was. She lived in his beach house with him and she had a credit card to shop and he bought her handbags from Louis Vuitton, a two carat tennis bracelet and matching earrings. She ignored that during the off season he traveled to California where he was from alone, for two months. She really didn't care. When he was in

Jacksonville he was with her and more importantly he took care of her. That is until she saw on the evening news that Detron had signed a hundred million dollar contract with the San Francisco team in a trade and was engaged to Gabriela, a reality TV Star he went to college with. She realized she was once again collateral damage with thousands of dollars' worth of handbags, clothes, shoes and jewelry. Before he left he gave her a new set of Louis Vuitton luggage worth almost ten thousand dollars and the receipts. Being a practical woman Chelsea knew she was returning it the next day for cash.

For four months until they evicted her she stayed in the beach house not hearing once from Detron. Nor did she try phoning him. The morning of the eviction she packed up her clothes, shoes, handbags and jewelry having the driver take her to a centrally located hotel in Jacksonville. She checked in to ALOFT hotel paying for three weeks. She knew her assets would carry her for several months if she were savvy. She wasn't going back to Detroit no matter what and at thirty one; she knew her prey would be different. Detron was her last baller.

SCENE TWO

Two days after moving into the hotel, Chelsea ventured out to Starbucks within walking distance. She wasn't a woman to throw pity parties and she wasn't in love with Detron. Her confession was she was tired of the hustle, the game. She was dressed down in jeans and a snug t-shirt with leather booties. Her long flowing weave had been exchanged for a short shoulder length bob in a more muted red and as always her face was done. Chelsea *knew* makeup enhanced her looks. People often told her she looked like Rosie Perez, the Latina actress. She didn't find that especially complimentary.

Feeling eyes on her after getting coffee and a scone and sitting near the window, Chelsea glanced up to find, soft brown eyes on her. They belonged to a woman who appeared to be in her forties with short curls, with brown skin, wearing a black maxi dress. There was something all-knowing in her eyes and she didn't look away when Chelsea met her eyes. On the table were a coffee cup, small laptop and folders. The woman smiled and stood, walking to Chelsea's table.

"Hello, I'm Ann Mitchell. I'm not a crazy; everyone in here can vouch for me." The woman laughed from deep in her throat, an almost sexy laugh. Chelsea was startled by the sound of it. "I'm approaching you because I just received a six week project for a local women's group. It involves lots of typing and pays well. Can you type?" The woman asked, those eyes never leaving Chelsea's face.

"I can type about sixty words a minute." Chelsea hadn't typed in years but knew she still could. Her aunt encouraged her to take office classes in high school and her one year in tech school. She chose bartending because it paid better and there were more men. "You don't even know me." The woman filled the air with more laughter.

"I don't and don't need to but I know you need a job, don't ask how, I just know things. So if you can type and need fifteen dollars an hour meet me here tomorrow at ten."

"Where will I work?" Chelsea had already calculated in her head and knew with what money she had the earnings would cover her room and board for two more months without having to sell anything else. That appealed to her.

"Wherever you're staying. I'll bring the boxes of typing, it's labeled and in order. You type and email to me after each project is done. Today is Friday, so I'll pay you each Friday. This can be our meeting spot. I require excellent work."

"Thank you, I can do that. My name is Chelsea Swift."

"Great. I'll see you here tomorrow." Ann walked to her table, gathered her things and made her way out, waving as she left. The barista, a young black woman, said in the nearly empty coffee house, "Ms. Ann is a real one. She got me in school and this job but she doesn't tolerate fools." Chelsea smiled slightly. She wasn't usually partial to women but there was something about Ann Mitchell, especially that laugh, it was from deep down, genuine and kind of bawdy.

~~YYYYY~~

Ann was pleased with Chelsea's work and told her on their first Friday meeting. She gave her a check for six hundred dollars and told her she always had work if needed and even more contacts.

"Who are you?" Chelsea asked.

"I'm Ann Mitchell; I'm married with grown sons, a semi-retired educator and counselor. I have also mentored hundreds of girls and women and have a nonprofit geared towards mentoring and education. Mostly, I'm a Black woman who gives a damn about her community. My life could have turned out many ways were it not for committed women who gave a damn. Who are you Chelsea Swift?"

Chelsea gave her a brief synopsis, mostly about what occurred with Detron and how she ended up at the hotel. She was unflinchingly honest.

"What do you want Chelsea?" The younger woman's face hardened a bit.

"Not to have to hustle so hard. I've been on the hustle most of my adult life and in and out of my aunt's home. She's the only stable one of my mom and the other aunts. She allowed me to live with her but pay my own way. I also never want to go back to Detroit. I like Jacksonville, it's big but slow and country, and I need that."

Ann knew the story, she heard it often, young attractive women who allowed men to fund them until either the funds ran out or the men unfunded them for younger, more attractive women. Ann guessed Chelsea as mid-thirties and was surprised she was thirty one. Her eyes and face spoke of lots of late nights and some hard living.
"Do you hustle people, Chelsea?" Ann asked softly.
"I have."
"Until that changes things will remain rocky. If you're interested in a place let me know. I know people with very nice studio apartments for a lot less per month than you pay weekly at that hotel. Of course, you'll have to make up your own bed."

By the beginning of the third week of working with Ms. Ann, Chelsea moved into a nice second floor studio in San Marco for seven hundred per month, there was a bedroom; bathroom, living and kitchen area with a small balcony and utilities were included. It was owned by an older woman and the four apartments were rented only to women and children. Chelsea loved the quiet, clean space. She worked for Ann four months before meeting Robert at a jazz bar downtown.

YYYYY

Robert surprised Chelsea by being excellent in bed. He was eleven years older at forty two and divorced with one son aged fifteen with his ex-wife and a twenty year old son with a girlfriend. He was paying child support for the former. He lived in a good sized fixer upper in a good neighborhood. She noted he was a frugal man and she liked that. He wasn't overly generous but she wanted to live in a home and some stability and Robert fit that bill. The eighty eight thousand he brought home annually wasn't football money but she knew that ship had sailed. They were a lot alike and she decided he would be her husband. She couldn't have children and that suited him, he hated supporting the ones he had. He was a transplant to Jacksonville the same as she was and his kids lived in Alabama. That suited her.

SCENE THREE

For almost two years things went well with Chelsea and Robert. She convinced him to sell the fixer upper and purchase a newer home with the proceeds and a mortgage. Robert wasn't thrilled about that but gave in. He had fallen in love with the quirky woman though suspected she didn't love him as much. She had gotten hired as a secretary earning mid five figures due to the work she did for Ann and Ann's recommendation. The only bone of contention was his family. She had met his parents and sister and didn't care for them. The feeling was mutual. They were too phony and churchy for her and they felt she was too worldly. The difference between them was minimal because they drank as much as she did but privately and Chelsea drank a lot. Her and Robert shared love for alcohol and Chelsea didn't believe in hiding anything. She was bold. She was also grateful they lived in Alabama and didn't visit. She rarely went with Robert when he visited. Initially he tried convincing her but came to accept it after an argument.

Robert I'm not going, your people are phony as hell and it's God this and God that but they gossip, do under the table things and drink in cute glasses. I'm not going through that shit. I don't ask you to go to Chicago and I'm not going to Alabama because they are all a bunch of Bamas. " She wanted to add and so is your ass.

"But you don't have any people except your Aunt and y'all ain't close."

"I'm closer to her than anybody but check this out, if I'm not running up there to see her who fed, clothed and sheltered me I'm not going there. My Aunt came here one time and treated you like a king. Your folks talk about old shit like I'm not even alive."

Robert had to accept the truth of that.

~~YYYYY~~

Three days before their second anniversary, Chelsea left work early not feeling well. She had a hard time adjusting to the intense heat the Florida summers brought and the air conditioning at her office went out. She was stunned when she walked inside at noon to find Robert on the sofa in his boxers watching ESPN. He jumped up, asking her why she was home.

"Why am I home? Why in the hell are you home?" She asked her eyes boring into him. He dropped down on the sofa, looking like balloon with the air punched out.

"I got laid off... they downsized and I was one of the first to go. I have twenty years of service as a computer tech and been with Xerox several but no degree and I'm a black man." Chelsea felt something bitter fill her and she rolled her eyes at the black man comment. She got tired of hearing that from Robert on his shortcomings as a father, how much his child support was or his job. It was his mantra. And that family of his enabled his shit.

Her immediate concern was the mortgage. Robert paid the thousand dollar mortgage, his child support, and gave her six hundred; she took care of electricity, food and other incidentals. She didn't have any debt and was actually saving money. She had no idea what he did with the rest of his earnings, other than liquor, expensive shoes and hats. They didn't travel or eat out much.

"Black man, what are you going to do because the mortgage is monthly? How much do you have saved?" She was literally hissing.

"A few hundred..." he said and she raced across the room and started pummeling him as if she were crazed. It was as if a tidal wave unleashed in her. He was finally able to control her, holding her until she collapsed on the sofa.

"How is that possible? After your bills you should have about twenty five hundred left each month, what in the hell did you spend sixty thousand dollars on over two years even deducting twenty for liquor, shoes and shit, where is the money?" With the six hundred he gave her and the additional four hundred monthly she added, her savings was almost thirty thousand. She hadn't purchased clothes since Detron left. Her closets were filled and she still had her earrings and bracelet. She promised she would never be broke again. She confessed that to a God she rarely talked to.

"They cut my hours to twenty five instead of forty and overtime a year ago." Tears of frustration flowed down Chelsea's cheeks. She wasn't one to cry but she couldn't control it. Robert reached for her but she smacked his hand away and grabbed her purse. She had to talk to Ms. Ann or she would explode or hurt Robert, bad. Ms. Ann surprised her by inviting her over. Ann rarely blurred lines and her home was mostly off limits. She also rarely visited homes of those she mentored unless they were underage.

~~YYYYY~~

Chelsea looked around Ms. Ann's home feeling the calming energy. There were lots of books, plants and the scent of lemongrass filled the spacious living room. The furnishings were mostly soft leather with lots of pillows and Asian rugs with black art. It looked like the woman.

"Your home is beautiful but I'm surprised to be here." Chelsea said. Ann smiled widely as she invited Chelsea to sit. She had tea and chicken salad prepared. Chelsea's stomach grumbled she hadn't eaten since breakfast at seven thirty. After serving herself she spilled what she learned about Robert.

"Ms. Ann, I could only wonder how long he was going to go without telling me and he was laying up on the couch instead of looking for another damn job. And don't mention for better or for worse... he should have told me." Ann felt for Chelsea, she personally would have likely taken her husband's head off for the same thing.

"I agree with you Chelsea and would like have reacted similarly. Why don't you have a joint account for shared bills?" Chelsea looked as if that had never occurred to her. She didn't know of anyone who did. Her aunt raised her to have her own and said she never let a man know how much she had.

"That never occurred to me. He paid what he paid and I paid what I paid and I told him before marrying him how much I required because he earned twice as much as I did. Ms. Ann, a year ago he should have told me about the hours cut and found another job or second job. I would never let him walk in to the lights being off or no food in the refrigerator. To me he's a damn liar."

"Not telling is a form of lying but for better or worse in *marriage* is a real thing Chelsea. Is the house behind?" Chelsea pulled out her phone and quickly checked. It was August and the last payment date was June 1st. They were two months behind. Her head started hurting and she felt nauseous. She was also angry for not checking behind him.

"It's two months behind. Ms. Ann, I'm going to pay that but I promise you I'm not providing a roof for a grown man. I know I've had arrangements with men but they weren't my husband. If he can't pay by September we have a problem. Chelsea is not doing it. No ma'am." Chelsea stared at her mentor in defiance. Ann threw up her hands.

"Oh, I understand. I'm with you on that but perhaps you can give him a bit more grace..."
"I really don't know." Chelsea said and meant it. "He lied for a whole damn year. That's a lot."
"That's honest. You've grown a lot since I met you. That woman I met in Starbucks dressed in tights with six hundred dollar booties would never have been paying utilities or buying groceries much less paying two months in back mortgage. I hope you see that." Chelsea's face colored at Ms. Ann's words.
"I do see that and I thank you. Ms. Ann, you don't *tell* any of us what to do but you say things and show things that resonate. You also work to make our lives better, like my job in a law office. I have changed but I'm not supporting a man Ms. Ann. It's not happening. I'm thirty three, he's forty five. No ma'am."
"I'm with you in all that." Ann hadn't cared for Robert but kept that to herself because when she met him she knew he was smitten with her young protégé and she knew Chelsea wasn't in love with him. She still wasn't. Robert reminded Ann of many men in third thirties and forties they wanted the most for the bare minimum and had no problem with being supported by their women as long as no one knew about it. Many bragged about what *they* had when they hadn't added a thing to it. Chelsea paid the two months and relaxed a bit eating her food and sipping her tea. Ann shared that her husband was in Atlanta for two days and

she couldn't go because earlier that day she had a
workshop.

SCENE FOUR

In October, Robert came up with enough to pay the mortgage though he still wasn't working and getting three hundred dollars per week in unemployment. Chelsea made clear when she returned from Ann's she was not paying past September and would find her own place if he didn't. The cable which he paid was cutoff and she left it off. She could care less about cable. She only liked movies and watched on her laptop in bed with Netflix and Hulu apps. She had also increased her savings by taking in typing clients for nights and weekends.

Robert went out daily as if he were looking for work but she didn't buy it, most job applications were done on the internet. Their sex life which was the one bright spot was nonexistent. Chelsea wasn't going to beg a man for dick. The final straw for her was the night Robert's mom called.

"Hello Chelsea. Robert told me y'all were struggling and I just called to say it takes two to make it nowadays. One salary isn't enough."

"Ma'am, you need to be saying that to your son. I don't know what you heard but I've never not worked since I knew him. In fact I work two jobs and pay all my parts."

"Sometimes a black man needs a little help..."

Chelsea couldn't control her snorting.

"Well you better help him then. I'm not his mama or that woman. A man who has twenty five years of experience can get a job. He just needs to stop

lying, get up off his ass and work. He's forty five and able. I'm not the one. Please from now on talk to your son and not me. Thank you." Chelsea said and hung up. An hour later, Robert walked in the room, his eyes blurry from drinking.
"Mama said you disrespected her." He slurred.
"She disrespected herself by calling me. You're her *child* I'm not."
"She was just trying to encourage us." Chelsea finally looked up from her computer.
"I don't want or need her encouragement Robert. I'm done. I'll give you fifteen thousand dollars to sign the house over to me or I'll buy my own."
"I put fifty in this house you wanted. I need thirty..."
"Fifteen or I'll get my own. I'm done." She said. Robert advanced towards the bed his fists balled up. Chelsea stared at him unblinking. Her eyes conveyed something that made him turn from her and leave the room.
Three weeks later, he signed the home over to her and she gave him a check. Two days after that he filled a small U-Haul with his things and moved to Alabama.

A Year Later....
Neither Robert nor Chelsea filed for divorce. Chelsea was working her two jobs and providing for herself. She had refinanced the house and

lowered her payments by two hundred dollars. She hadn't dated but was considering it but fully on her terms. At thirty four she vowed to never depend on anyone again. She still spoke to Ms. Ann weekly. Robert was staying in a small trailer on his family property and doing temporary work.

BOOSTING

Cassandra was born into a family of boosters or in non-hood parlance, thieves. Her mom Emily and three older sisters, Mary, Martha and Sara were thieves, they stole clothes, jewelry, perfume, handbags and other things women loved and sold them. By the time Emily was thirty four and pregnant with Cassandra, the older girls were fifteen, fourteen, and thirteen and were professional thieves. They lived in a big, rambling house Emily's grandmother left her and it was beautiful inside, furnished with money from their profession and full of things they boosted. Emily was taught by her mom and aunt to boost but raised by her grandmother who wanted nothing to do with the family business but she couldn't keep Emily away. By the time Emily had Mary at nineteen her mom and grandmother were dead and her aunt in prison. But she kept the legacy going. At age thirty five when she gave birth to Cassandra by Slim Jones, the father of all her girls, she vowed that baby would never be in the game. But some things even well-meaning mothers couldn't control...

Scene One

Emily gave Cassandra a huge twelfth birthday
party. Her baby was going to eighth grade and
Emily was proud. All of the girls were good
students in spite of their other proclivities but
Mary, Martha nor Sara who were now twenty
seven, twenty six and twenty five ever wanted
college. They all had jobs supplemented by their
real incomes and lived in their own homes. It was
only Emily and Cassandra at home. Emily at forty
six no longer *worked.* She had money stashed and
Slim at fifty who owned a mechanic shop had
always provided for her and his girls. He just
wasn't the marrying or settling down type. He was
a come in and leave the money on the table man
and was out. Rumor was Slim had other daughters
in Georgia but Emily could care less.

"Mom and Dad this is the best party." Cassandra
said. There were a few friends there but mostly her
sisters and older people. Emily didn't believe in
her kids dealing with too many people because as
she said, "They stayed in your damn business."

Slim grinned, sitting in his reserved lounge chair in
the corner with a black baseball cap sitting jauntily
on his head. Slim wasn't traditionally handsome
but had smooth black skin and a sexy grin which
along with his tall, slim body and hefty wallet
attracted women. The women always looked like

Emily, light brown skin with abundant curves and lots of curly hair. They also had to be great cooks and clean. His girls with Emily all had her curves on a lesser scale and hair but were all stunning with his darker skin, tall frame and high cheekbones. Men looked but nobody messed with anything that belonged to Slim, including Emily.

"Anything for you baby girl." He said. Emily rolled her eyes because Slim funded it but she did all the work. Cassandra was spoiled by her and everyone knew it. Cassandra loved being the center of attention and spoiled but more than anything she wanted to be like her mom and sisters. She remembered them coming in with great hauls of clothes, jewelry and perfume. They were giddy and talking about how much money they would make. At nine Cassandra asked when they would teach her and Emily smacked her, saying, "Never, this ain't for you! Go to your room." Emily was adamant about that but Cassandra was already taking things. She had a bigger plan.

The doorbell rang and Cassandra raced to get it. She started giggling when she saw her mentor, Ms. Ann with a huge bag. Emily had asked Ann to mentor Emily after she showed interest in boosting. Emily had been tutored by Ann as an eighth grader when Ann was a senior in high school. She hadn't cared much for her then and felt Ann was forced on her by her grandma but she admitted she was helped with her grades and testing. Emily immediately thought of her when Cassandra needed mentoring not tutoring. Ann was a certified counselor for girls and women.

"Hey Ms. Ann, thanks for coming." Cassandra said, wrapping her arms around the woman who spoke straight to her. Emily waved from her chair and Slim quickly stood, straightening his hat. Emily snorted. Cassandra and Slim acted like the damn woman was royalty. Slim was about twelve years older than Ann but knew her people and what she was about in the community.

"Hey baby. Happy birthday." Ann said before turning to Emily and Slim. "Hey Emily. Curtis, you're looking mighty dapper." She said. Emily winked and Slim smiled cockily. Very few people other than his mama called him Curtis. Ann was one.

"Hey beautiful; It's always good to see you. Can I get you a drink or some food? We had cake already."

"I would love cake and water. Thank you." Ann said, sitting in an armchair near Emily. Cassandra opened the bag and pulled out things Ms. Ann knew Cassandra loved, books by R. L. Stine, Beverly Cleary books that Ann once loved, saltwater taffy and jolly rancher candies and a gift certificate to Waldenbooks bookstore." Cassandra was thrilled and hugged Ann in thanks as Slim returned with cake and a glass of water. Cassandra chattered as Ann ate her food about the books to her parents and mentor. Emily got up and filled two take home trays with food for Ann and her husband. Slim joined her in the kitchen.

"Em, Ann is good people."

"I know or she wouldn't be counseling my baby. Women like her just make me uncomfortable. All elegant and educated but regular; I prefer the stuck-up heffas, you can just ignore them but her ass is genuine." Emily said, placing the food nicely in the containers.

Emily would never admit it but she regretted not going to college because she had been as smart as Cassandra but almost thirty years earlier she was making a thousand dollars a week after giving the girls their cut and her friend who taught school earned four hundred and fifty. Besides her mom wasn't hearing it. When her mom died she was nineteen and pregnant with Mary so there was no turning back. She earned a lot of money and was smart with it. She did the same with her older daughters as her mom had with her, when Cassandra came she wanted better because by thirty five she knew better. It was a miracle neither her nor the girls had records. Slim said it was

because they were pretty, smart and weren't ghetto
acting. She knew that was true. Though they were
still boosting they all worked and carried
themselves well.

"Em, she's a good lady who gives a damn." Slim
said sliding the plates Emily filled into a grocery
bag.

"I know." Emily said, grabbing the bag and
heading to the living room.

Ann thanked Emily and Slim and hugged
Cassandra before going home. Her mouth watered
at the scent of garlic fried chicken and smoked
curry steak that Emily was famous for. She knew
there would also be two vegetables cooked
perfectly. Emily cooked like a chef. Ann shook
that thought away. Emily was a grown woman
who seemed to love her life.

SCENE TWO

A week after her party Cassandra went to read to Ms. Bernice at the nursing home. Ms. Ann required service in exchange for mentoring. Cassandra didn't mind and Ms. Bernice was going to be her first boost. Ms. Bernice was in her eighties and forgetful. She also had hundreds of dollars inside the big old bible Cassandra read from. The last time she was there, there were thirteen one hundred dollar bills throughout the pages, mostly near the back. Cassandra only read from Proverbs and Psalms because they made sense to her. She had taken one bill two weeks earlier and nothing happened. This time she was going to take three, maybe four.

"Hey Ms. Bernice." She said cheerily, walking into the room. Ms. Bernice turned her eyes to Cassandra looking with her grey eyed stare.

"Who are you?" The old woman asked. Cassandra picked up the Bible and sat on the foot of the bed. Ms. Bernice was tiny; her feet didn't even reach the foot. She always smelled like rose powder which Cassandra liked. Many old people smelled funny.

"Ms. Bernice, I'm Cassandra, Ms. Ann's student."

Cassandra opened the Bible and read Psalm 100

1

A psalm of thanksgiving.

Shout joyfully to the LORD, all you lands;
2

Serve the LORD with gladness;
Come before him with joyful song.
3

*Know that the LORD is God,
He made us, we belong to him,
We are his people, the flock he shepherds
4

Enter his gates with thanksgiving,
His courts with praise.
Give thanks to him, bless his name
5

Good indeed is the LORD,
His mercy endures forever,
His faithfulness lasts through every generation

Ms. Bernice listened as Cassandra read, her eyes
closed as she always did. Afterwards Cassandra sat

with her a few minutes before making sure her
water glass was filled and two sugar cookies were
on a plate near the glass. She was supposed to stay
thirty minutes but Ms. Bernice always fell asleep.
Cassandra opened the Bible, took three hundreds
and slid them in her jeans pocket before placing
the Bible on the small table near the window. She
glanced at Ms. Bernice before grabbing her book-
bag and heading for the door. She was stopped by
the nurse on duty at the door. A tall black lady
everyone called Nurse Barb. Barb was blocking
the doorway.

"Little girl, I saw you take that money. Follow me,
I'm calling Ann." Cassandra's eyes widened and
she tried to push past Barb but Barb caught her
arm and pulled her to the office, closing the door.
She quickly phoned Ann, telling her what
happened. Cassandra dropped into the chair,
kicking the carpet with her shoes. She didn't want
Ms. Ann to come. Anyone but her.

Ann arrived within thirty minutes. Nurse Barb
made Cassandra pull the folded bills from her
pockets and hand them to her mentor. Ann
flinched. Cassandra refused to meet Ann's eyes or
cry.

"Cassandra, why did you do this?" Ann asked.
"You don't need money." Cassandra shrugged,
refusing to answer.

"Young lady you better open your mouth and speak to me." Ann said. "Not only have you been barred from here for stealing but others may not be allowed because of you. Open your mouth and speak!"

"It was in there and I wanted it, so I took it." Cassandra said defiantly, still not meeting Ann's eyes but she spoke the truth. She wanted it.

"We cannot take things that aren't ours just because we want it Cassandra Jones. You know that. You could go to jail." Ann said.

"I'm twelve. They will release me to my mom or dad." A chill ran up Ann's spine. The child was entitled and spoiled and had seen too much in her young life.

"Yes, you're probably right but no one gets away with anything forever." Ann said. Cassandra finally looked up and smiled, saying, "Some do."

Ann froze. She knew she meant Emily. Emily was an infamous for having stolen untold amounts and never doing jail time. Ann knew Emily paid greatly for her choices and one payment was a defiant twelve years old but she was too sad to try to explain it that day. Nurse Barb interjected.

"Listen, smart mouth, if it wasn't for this lady I would call the cops and let you find out firsthand but never come near here again or I'm calling the law. Ann, get her out of here."

Ann and Cassandra were silent on the drive to Emily's home. Cassandra hurried out of the car but Ann got out and followed her. Emily was on the porch and immediately sensed trouble.

"Ann, what's going on?" Emily asked.

"Cassandra tell your mom what happened." Cassandra lifted her chin, facing her mom.

"I took money from Ms. Bernice Bible and..." Before she could finish her statement Emily jumped and punched her and pummeled her several times. It took Ann several minutes to react, she was so shocked. She tried pulling Emily away but she was swinging on her daughter who was yelling and trying to cover her head. Slim raced outside and grabbed Emily who looked deranged.

"I didn't raise you to steal Cassandra Jones. I'll beat the skin off you first." Emily shrieked. Her hair and eyes were wild as Slim held her. Cassandra's face was red and bruised from the pummeling.

"Sure you did Mama." Cassandra said calmly, racing off the porch. Slim released his girlfriend and chased after his daughter. Emily dropped down on the floor, sobbing and Cinnamon joined her, wrapping her arms around her.

"Ann, I didn't want that for her. I did and gave her everything..." Emily said through sobs.

"I know but kids often do what they want, not what we say. She's a good girl and let's hope this will scare her straight." Emily pulled away and sat up, brushing away her tears.

"I doubt it. The older girls all told me Cassandra idolized me and what I'm known for. I never hid what I did or what the girls did but Ann by the time I had her I wasn't the same mom or woman. I made them work and thought if I didn't with Cassandra... I guess it's what y'all call generational curses. My mom died younger than I am now from too much alcohol and no rules. I tried with Cassandra." Emily sounded completely broken.

"Emily, you are still trying. You just can't be as indulgent with her and it's never too late to set up boundaries. I'll be there for her as always."
Emily's eyes met Ann's.

"Why?"

"Because I care Emily and Cassandra is worth it. I honestly believe everyone is worth being given chances until they figure it out. Not all do but I believe until the end. I grew up with a mom who drank too much and was married to an abusive man but who still had rules and boundaries for me and expectations of me. I had to do well in school, work and volunteer. My life wasn't charmed. I could have gotten a completely different life but for mom, my aunts, godmother and teachers. I had a village I want to be part of Cassandra's."

"Thank you. Please come inside I need coffee. You want some?"

"I would love some."

Slim caught up to his daughter and allowed her to cry in his arms.

"Baby girl, your Mama loves you and you don't have to take from nobody. You hurt Em today and she got too mad. I want you to come home, wash up and stay away from your mom the rest of the night. I'll stay over and talk to her."

"Yes sir."

Emily and Ann were drinking coffee when Slim returned with Cassandra. He made her apologize to

Ann and her mom before doing as he told her. She did and rushed to her room.

"Em, give her the night." Slim said. "I'll be here with y'all, I'm going to fix her plate after she washes up. Thanks Ann for being there." Emily nodded tiredly.

"No problem. I've run up in drug houses and worse." Ann said.

"Oh I know you're about that life ma'am and we appreciate you. Y'all need refills?" Both women held out their cups to him.

Cassandra was sleeping fully dressed when Slim took her food in to her. He slid off her shoes and covered her up. He walked in the hallway and stopped to listen.

"Emily, all you have is today forward. Talk to her about what you want for her. Share honestly why you did what you did and why you don't think it's for her. She needs to hear more than because I said so. If you can handle it, take her to see your incarcerated aunt. You both can get through this." Ann said softly. Slim held his breath, hoping Emily didn't cuss the woman out.

"Do you think that will work Ann?"

"I do. Kids crave truth and discipline though they don't know it and from parents. I can speak on how wrong what she did is but I can't tell her your story and most importantly I'm not the woman she loves and admires most. Emily, this isn't about three hundred dollars but how much she wants to be you. You are her model for life. Share you with her and turn this around. You're more than that one little thing." Tears spilled down Emily's cheek because she felt like she *was* that one thing.

"Thank you but I need backup."

"I'm your backup woman but it's going to cost you more of this delicious coffee and those garlic chicken wings. I had to stop my man from doing a garlic chicken drive by. Woman, you're a chef." Genuine laughter flew from Emily's throat as she visibly relaxed.

And Ann Mitchell, you're a genius. Slim thought before returning to the dining room.

Emily walked Ann to her car and for the first time hugged her.

Slim hugged her when she walked back inside, her eyes red and tired.

"Em, you're a good Mama. Do what Ann said and give it time. Our baby is a good one. She's just heard too much and thinks it's all fun and games. Now she knows."

"It's my fault. She sees how I live and her sisters and she's us. We make it look like fun and games. It was Slim honestly but I have regrets and I told the other girls to roll out. They will or won't."

"They're grown, they work and it's their choice now. Let's take this day by day. I'll tell the older girls to stop talking around their sister but they ain't around much anyway. Emily, we all got dirt. Now go wash up and I'll take care of you after I put up the food and stuff."

"Slim, it's just six thirty."

"Woman, I know what time it is now go... just be glad she got caught young and that Ann was there."

"Oh, I am..."

SCENE THREE

It was more than a month before Emily discussed her life and past with Cassandra. The next morning she told her she was fully restricted.

"I'll be taking you to and from school, I will sit in on your sessions with Ms. Ann and there will be no meals out, shopping or anything like that." Emily said firmly. Cassandra opened her mouth to speak but Emily told her to shut it. Cassandra glanced at Slim who sat with them but he reinforced Emily with his silence.

It was almost as difficult for Emily as for Cassandra because she had to get up and go out twice per day and that wasn't her norm. She usually got up with Cassandra but was back in bed after the bus left at seven thirty until almost noon. Three days per week after school she and Cassandra usually tried a new restaurant and went shopping or hanging out. Emily treated Cassandra like her friend. It was difficult sitting in the sessions. Ann was honest and forthright which caused Emily to realize how little she knew about many things. Things she was never taught. The most difficult was Cassandra barely talked to her or watched shows with her in the evenings.

The tipping point for them both came when five weeks after Cassandra's incident; Sara was arrested at work and paraded in cuffs on television. It seemed that other than boosting Sara had been stealing from the business she worked for as a finance secretary. The company found discrepancies and monitored her for six months. She had taken more than twelve thousand dollars. Tears poured down Emily's face as she saw her beautiful and elegantly dressed daughter walk in cuffs with her head held high, smiling for the cameras like a movie star. Emily knew she created that ego and pride. She always told the girls when they started working to never poop where they ate, meaning to not take money from employers or date men they worked for or with.

"She's so pretty." Emily heard behind her and turned to see Cassandra in her pajamas. She beckoned for her daughter who came and sat next to her. "Mama, is she going to prison?"

"Baby, she might. It depends on her plea, what they got on her and the judge. She doesn't have a record and I'm going to call my lawyer. Cassandra that's why I was so upset with you, I don't want that for you. I was wrong to bring the older girls into it. I started with mom and auntie when I was younger than you and so did your sisters. For all of us it was easy money and fun. We were pretty women and well spoken, no one suspected us but many knew and remained quiet. People shopped from us like it was a store. I was raised to believe because the white man stole from us to get it back from them. I'm not sure I ever stopped feeling that way, I just got tired. I had them at nineteen, twenty and twenty one but was thirty five when I had you and was no longer out there much... it's illegal and can lead to this. Cassandra be better than us, than me." Emily said. She kissed her daughter on the forehead and went to call Slim and her attorney.

~~YYYYYY~~

The next morning Emily received a call from Slim that Sara was released and was going to plead for probation. She was shocked at how quickly that worked.

"Slim, how is that possible, no bond or nothing?" Slim hesitated but knew he had to tell the truth.

"Em, she was involved with the man she worked for. He's a rich White man with a wife and money. He got her the deal quickly to keep her mouth shut." Emily swallowed down sadness. Sara had broken both rules but it seemed to be working in her favor. "Sara always looks out for Sara." He said.

Emily knew that was true. Sara was the youngest for thirteen years. She was also reckless and not prone to listening unless it suited her.

"Did you talk to her?"

"No, she doesn't want to talk to either of us. She's home and seems unconcerned Em. This is even more reason to protect Cassandra."

"I know."

Emily told Cassandra a cleaned up version, leaving out the affair.

"Mama, I'm good." Cassandra said, wrapping her arms around her mom. Seeing her sister in cuffs touched something inside her.

~~ΥΥΥΥΥΥ~~

Six years later Emily, Slim and Ann stood with Cassandra in the airport. She decided to go in the Air Force. She had done dual enrollment in high school and gotten a high school diploma and associates degree two weeks apart. Everyone wanted her to go to college but she decided she needed to get further away. Her first assignment after basic training and sixteen weeks of advanced training would be London. Emily was sad but proud. Mary was no longer boosting but married and pregnant, Martha was still in the game and working, Sara was working in her own business *Sara Styles* as a makeup artist and the mom to five year old Julian who everyone suspected was for her former boss. It was also suspected she had been paid well for her silence and Julian's care.

"She will do well." Ann said.

"She will." Slim agreed. Emily knew they were right. She also knew it would be a long time before she saw her Cassandra again because to truly flourish she had to get away from all of them. What no one knew but her and Cassandra was three pair of her most expensive diamond earrings were in Cassandra's bag and she hadn't given them to her.

Knowing Better, Doing Better

Angelia Vernon Menchan
Has ISH Too

I had to grow out of being a mad woman. I started being mad young and for years and years and years, it sustained me. I actually equated mad with strength and if someone had told me in my twenties and thirties I would have told them they was lying, at that time my anger was my strength.

How could I be mad? I was a good person who would do anything for anyone, and often before they even asked and mad, shoot, I tell people off, I don't hold mad, it comes out.

Ha!

It did come out but in no way did it alleviate the anger that had been banked inside me and festering most of my life. I couldn't admit why I was angry, and as a result, I couldn't deal with the anger living inside me. I didn't see it all at once but signs of it started revealing itself over the years.

I recall an incident living in Germany when a good friend of mine was accused of rape. We were all aghast and wanted to do whatever we could in his defense. He was the third soldier the woman accused and we didn't need to see another career ruined. However, when they were collecting

witnesses, no one ever asked me. I was surprised
by that because he had visited my home and I felt
we were close. I asked our supervisor for the day
off and he told me I wasn't a witness.

"Huh?"

"He didn't add you to the witness list Angelia. No
one thought it was a good idea."

"Why is that?" I asked.

"Because you are a bit of a wild card and no one
knows what you might say or do if you are angry."

My head snapped back at his words and I could not
and did not see myself in that way. However, I was
raging inside at the idea they had discussed me and
thought of me that way. I pretended not to care and
ended up called as the last witness of the day.

Afterwards we were at lunch and I asked him
about what I had been told. He didn't really look in
my eyes but he was honest.

"Sis, you know I love you but you go off on people
and I didn't need you going off on the witness
stand and you went off when I told you."

"I never thought you did that." I snapped.

"Yes you did. You believed me but you went off
because I was a married man and should not have
been messing with that girl. You let me know in

the harshest terms. Sis, I love you and you are a good woman but you go in."

I shrugged off his words but they pierced my bones. I felt it deep inside and it wasn't something my husband, sister and others hadn't said to me in different ways. His eyes searched mine and I put on a smile and sucked it down. Instead of actually saying, you hurt my feelings, I dealt with it by burying it deep down and allowing it to meld with the other anger.

~~YYYYY~~

By the time I was in my mid-thirties my imbedded anger started to deal with me. I was working at the time in a high-energy job, and there were myriad management issues concerning employees and I was the buffer for those. I wasn't feeling well, made myself an appointment, and was shocked when my blood pressure registered 148/99. Prior to that, I had been proud of my low blood pressure and now it was extremely elevated. Of course, I went through a series of tests and appointments; and at thirty-six ended up on medication. I started doing all the physical things that would help but to no avail.

One night I unleashed on my then preteen eldest son and almost collapsed from the exertion. He was in that 'I am going to drive my mom insane,' age and it was working. I sent him and his younger brother to their rooms, and was lying on the sofa when my husband arrived. I must have looked really awful because he sat down beside me, touching me to see if I were feverish. I told him what happened and his words rained down on me.

"Baby, you let them, all of us make you too mad. You try to be everything to everyone and you can't. You are also on a rapid career track and its taking a toll on you. They have you working on holidays and they call you at midnight when the machines go down. Something has to give."

I burst into tears because there was that angry thing again and he was right. For most of my twenties and early thirties my life was devoted to him and our sons and instead of careers; I had jobs for the most part. The few ladders I climbed, I had to climb down from when it was time to go. Though I pretended it didn't bother me, it really did. I felt I was being cheated and didn't know how to articulate that without sounding 'unwife-like' or 'bad-motherish.' That was at the root of my issues: I was mired down in perfectionism and not admitting what truly bothered me but blowing up at infractions that weren't that big a deal. I recall getting off the sofa and making my way upstairs to pray. I prayed very perfunctorily at best during that time of my life and church wasn't in the equation. But, that day I talked to God asking for guidance.

It didn't come immediately but it started to trickle in. We were a few months from leaving and I gave my notice at a job I actually hated and started focusing on my health by riding my bike and walking.

I also started to consciously think about what I was going to say and how I was going to say it, realizing everything didn't need responding to or even saying. And by consciously I mean I literally woke up speaking those words to myself. It was amazing how well it works when it becomes part of your routine. I was literally able to talk myself out of an argument or a response.

When we moved, I also immediately enrolled in college, something I had put off doing for years to get an advanced degree and because I had saved enough to do it and still contribute.

I must be honest and say initially, my folks didn't respond well to my changes. They saw my not going off or commenting on everything they did as not caring. I can recall my husband saying he was going to do something that would have previously angered me, and I responded with 'Okay but count me out.'

My eldest son who is one of the most brilliant minds I know was a mediocre student who I felt for years I could punish or push into excellence and when he brought home his report card and it was less than stellar, I recalled handing it back to him and telling him to have his dad sign it. It still makes me chuckle that he asked if I were okay.

I wasn't at all okay but I was working on becoming okay as a human being and that started with working on me. It also meant letting some things go. If my eldest wanted to be mediocre, ultimately he would have to live with it. Sometimes the struggle was and is real but every morning, just as I started doing years ago, I talk myself into conscious decisions to do, say and be better, especially since aging, being taught and accepting the truth demands it. Every day is a step.

The Boys We Thought We Loved

Angelia Vernon Menchan

I recall the first boy I was truly enamored with I was twelve and he was probably fifteen. He worked behind the meat counter at a local grocery store and he was so handsome. I would often go to that store several times a day just to see him and flirt. I had filled out nicely and boys and men were paying close attention to the curves. So was my mom actually, and her spies.

I recall one day I rolled my jean shorts up to my crotch and tied my shirt around my waist, baring my belly. Now you had to see me. I was five feet nine inches with legs like a racehorse and yards of flying hair. Oh yeah, I unraveled my braids too. Anyway, I sashayed in that store and walked up to the meat counter, ordering a pound of ham and another of cheese. Mom always left money home on Friday for me to get food for sandwiches. I whipped my hair around and I know CH was checking me out. What I didn't know was others were as well. After getting my food, I went home and rolled those shorts down, did my chores and prepared sandwiches for my sister and me.

About two hours later my mom burst in the door and yanked me out the chair, looking me over.

"I heard you took your little hot ass over to the store half naked. What were you trying to prove? Do you know there are grown men who will ruin a girl like you?" She dragged me into the room and forced me to look at myself in the mirror.

"Look at you. You look ten in the face but that body and skin looks like a woman. Angel, do not throw yourself away on some nigger who won't care a damn about you." I heard her but I didn't care what she was saying. I wanted CH to like me and see me.

After that, I became sneakier and he would often meet me on the way from school and walk me almost home. One day he placed his lips on mine and I thought I would faint dead away. He literally taught me how to kiss that day. My almost thirteen-year-old body was in love. He told me to come to his house the next morning, everyone would be gone and he knew my mom worked on Saturday mornings. I agreed and raced home, my heart thumping in my chest. I was going to become a woman, I knew it. It was a month from my thirteenth birthday.

But that day as in many times in my life, God intervened and changed the course of my life. That evening after doing chores and eating, we went outside and started playing football of all things with the neighborhood boys and I ended up falling and breaking my leg. My mom came home and rushed me to the hospital and for the rest of winter break, which occurred that day I was at home with my leg set and healing. Of course, I didn't go to CH's house or the store.

When we returned to school, I was hobbling along and was confronted by a girl who it turns out was CH's girlfriend.

"You need to stay away from my man." She said, getting in my face.

"Who is your man?" I asked bewildered.

"CH is my man and I'm pregnant." I was sickened because we were in eighth grade, I wasn't quite thirteen and I knew she was fourteen and her being pregnant scared me literally. I was thinking if I had gone to his house, I would likely be pregnant. I was literally scared straight. I knew he didn't just want me to come over for more kisses.

I walked away from her and went about my business. I only went to the grocery store when I had to and I ignored him. He tried and tried but to me he stopped existing. God saved my life because years later, he ended up dying violently leaving behind several fatherless children. His girlfriend from the eighth grade had several kids for several guys after him. She had actually been a smart girl with good grades who gave up her future before realizing she had one.

My second enamored was a couple of years after the CH incident. I was best friends with his sister and had a huge crush on him. He was much older and treated me like a kid sister. I just did everything I could to be in his presence. He was fine, handsome and fine. He would often hangout with us when he came by to visit his mom and I was always in his line of sight. I didn't say much but I loved how he looked at me and one day he told me, "You are way too young and your mom would kill me."

Not long after that, I moved and didn't hear of him for years other than that he was involved in illegal activities. One night in high school, I ran into him at a football game and he approached me, still as handsome as ever and asked me out. By then I wasn't the same girl and my tastes in men had evolved though he was still hellaciously fine. Lord. I remember our conversation.

"You said I was too young for you." I said.

"Yea but you are all grown up now. I waited for you."

"Right. Where did you wait and with whom?" I said saucily. He laughed at me.

"You have become quite sophisticated haven't you?" he said, assessing me. I was dressed in my requisite blue jeans, button shirt and loafers at that time with my hair in a huge falling afro. He of course was dressed like the dirty west side in slacks, a leather jacket and cap. "My sister says you are in high school and taking college courses."

"I am." I said.

"You are so sexy with all that white girl clothing and talk. I should have taken it when I had a chance." I laughed and walked away with my cousin. I realized later, he probably could have taken it if he had tried back then, but for whatever reason I was grateful for his integrity at that time and my having a chance to grow up.

~~YYYYY~~

The first boy I loved, I didn't think I loved but I knew he loved me. We dated for a year and a half and I broke up with him. He took me to my first sweetheart dance, my first prom and many first outings. We spent many hot and heavy sessions kissing and touching and he was an amazing gift giver but I still broke up with him and stayed broke up for years. As a side note, a very important one, he never pressed me for sex and we didn't have any. We did, as I mentioned, kiss a lot and touch even more.

Years later after having dating having other dating experiences, I often thought of him and how he treated me until the night he showed up on my doorstep, asking to talk to me. We had several hours' of long conversation that night and went on a date a week later… when he finally kissed me, I fled from the car as if someone had shot me from a cannon. I am telling you, seeing sparks really does occur, and thirty-nine years later, thirty-eight years married, he can still shoot me from cannon…with his kisses.

The moral of this story, if there is any, is there will be those who fascinate us, fill us with desire and promises but if we pay close attention God will always send us the signs. God did not want me the pregnant middle-school girlfriend of CH or the ride or die chick of the next guy who became a drug kingpin before dying early and he sent me signs along the way that I actually had enough sense to heed. He then sent me the man in the form of a boy who treated me as God wanted me to be treated, and when I messed that up or maybe I didn't because we were both so young, he seasoned us both and sent him back to me when we were both ready. I am so grateful for all the boys I loved.

This is one of my first published stories… it has been out of print several years but fit the theme, so I am sharing it.

Angelia

SEPARATE LOVE LIVES

"I am about to go out to be with my lover, my husband is already out with his. What in the world are we doing?" Gloria silently asked as she paced around her spacious bedroom. She had been asking herself the same thing for months.

Plopping down on the edge, of her huge bed, she about how she and her husband Tyrone had started living this life, the life of an open marriage. She was getting dressed to meet her man. Tyrone was probably already in the throes of passion with his woman of the month. Standing up she started pacing again. She looked at her beautiful surroundings, acknowledging internally that all appearances indicated they had an ideal life. The reality though, was something else altogether.

They were in a second marriage for both. They'd been married fifteen years. Glo had a grown daughter from her first marriage, Ty had two grown sons with his first wife Veronica, Glo and Ty had a fourteen year old daughter, together. He was an executive with the local utility company and she sold real estate. They lived in a lovely home and attended one of the mega churches that were springing up all over town. They even had an excellent sex life, but she was having a fling and so was he. They had their life together and they had their alternative lives. After all this time, Gloria was trying to figure out why they were living separate love lives.

When Glo and Ty met sixteen years earlier, she was a thirty-three year old unhappily married woman with a thirteen-year old daughter. She had gotten married her third year of college because she had gotten pregnant. Getting married, if pregnant was what the daughter of a preacher did in those days. She had not been in love with her boyfriend Wayne and he had not been in love with her. They were just having sex and got caught and had to do the right thing. They had both come from families who demanded it and they'd complied.

By the time she met Ty, Glo had been very lonely for years. She had recently started selling real estate and was trying to find herself. She wasn't sure why she and Wayne were still married, because they had never fallen in love. The two of them had spent the past thirteen years going through the motions. He worked and provided while she raised their daughter, Maya. She had gone back to school to get her real estate license a couple of years ago. They did routine family stuff together, had sex occasionally and went their separate ways the rest of the time. She knew her husband was as lonely and as miserable as she was, but like her he thought all married people were miserable, that is just how it was.

Glo met Ty the second time she went out on her own to sell a house. She was supposed to meet a man and his wife to show a house. She had been told that they were in their late thirties and had recently won the lottery and wanted to purchase their dream house. Glo was very excited, because if she sold this one she would get her first real paycheck. Seven percent of five hundred thousand dollars was not bad.

Arriving at the property she noticed a tall man standing alone on the porch. She was a little anxious because she had been warned as a female that if she were meeting a man alone she should always have someone accompany her. As she approached the house, she noticed he was a very handsome man with a cocky arrogant look. He was average height, about five feet-ten inches, but very muscular and stocky. He had dark brown skin with short shiny black hair. He also had one of those mustaches that she fondly referred to as Black Clark Gables, thinly shaved, black and shiny. That mustache sat right above real nice, firm thick lips, a weakness of hers. Glo thought, *"Now why the heck am I thinking of that man's lips?"*

When she reached him, she noticed he smelled divine just like soap, toothpaste, and Polo cologne. Reaching for her, he took her hand in his, while looking her over from head to toe. She snatched her hand away, unprofessionally.

"Hello Mr. Williams, you are very early, I was trying to get here before you did."
 He continued to check her out.

"I am always on time Gloria. The early bird always gets the worm."

For some reason she flirted with him, even though his look irritated her.

"Who wants worms?"
 He laughed.

"Beautiful and sassy, I like that. I could really get to like you Miss Lady."

"That is Mrs. Lady to you, Mr. Williams." She blushed, thinking, *"Now where the heck did that come from?"*

She felt heated because it had been years since anyone had called her beautiful or since she had felt that way. Glo was 5 '6" tall and wore a size twelve. She was quietly proud of her new body because for years she had been stick thin. Once she turned thirty, she had gone from a size 6 to a size 12 and according to the few comments she had received the pounds were all in the right places. All of her friends had spent their lives trying to lose weight and she had always wanted to gain some. Her husband Wayne was the only person who seemed displeased with her weight. He felt everyone should be bone thin.

She had a very conservative look, suits with simple pumps or loafers. She had shoulder length braids because they were easy and could be styled in different ways. Her skin was pecan brown, clear and didn't require much makeup, other than lipstick. Intellectually, she knew she was attractive, but her heart had never convinced her to accept that. Her husband had never called her beautiful, ever.

Remembering her mission, Glo asked, "Where is your wife?"

"One of our sons isn't feeling well. Veronica is at home with him. You can show me the house. My wife has already seen it. This meeting is pretty much a formality."
He sounded very businesslike. Glo was intrigued by how easily he switched gears.

He followed her from room to room.

"We'll take it. I will get with you in a couple of days to finalize the paperwork. Veronica will be with me on that occasion. I need to get back to work."

Grabbing her hand again this time he was actually stroking it. Glo snatched her hand back as though burned.

"I didn't realize you worked. I thought you guys had won the lottery?"

"Of course I work. I'm only thirty-seven years old. Besides, we only got a couple million dollars after taxes. We have enough to buy this house, to save for the boys 'college, and have some money to live on. I have to work to maintain. I don't believe in acting rich without being rich."

She looked at him in admiration because she knew many people would have quit work immediately after receiving two million dollars. They would have financed the house and spent the rest. A few years later they would have been dead broke with nothing to show for it. She thought his wife was a lucky woman, one other reason being the way her hand had felt in his.

When they walked to their cars he shocked her. "You know I am going to make love to you right? So just go back to your world, Mrs. Lady and think about that. It is going to happen." He walked to his truck, got in and drove away saluting her.

She felt scared and excited. She got into her car and drove away listening to CeCe Winans. She was thinking, "I don't know who he thinks he is. As soon as I get my check for thirty five g's I won't have to see his arrogant ass again." She smiled to herself, because she sure wanted to see him again.

A few days later she met with him and Mrs. Veronica Williams. She was impressed by how pretty she was. She was an almond-colored sister with short hair streaked with four shades of brown. Her makeup and clothes were flawless. She was dressed way too provocatively, in Glo's opinion for ten o'clock in the morning in her light peach mini dress and four inch black and peach shoes, but she looked good in it. She was probably a size ten, with an extraordinarily curvy body. All of her curves and cleavage was exposed to the world. Her demeanor was as arrogant as her husband's. She didn't say a word to Glo or even look her way.

Glo could tell Ty was real proud of the way she looked, as though it were a reflection on him. She also noticed they didn't have any more spark between them than she and Wayne had. For some reason Glo found this thrilling. When all of the paperwork was done, Veronica stood up to leave.

"Tyrone I 'm going. I'll see you later at the house." She flounced out of the house. There were no hugs, kisses, nothing. She got in her red Acura, speeding off, dirt flying behind the car.

Ty turned to Glo, "Get ready beautiful, I'm taking you to lunch to celebrate the new house and your commission. You can even pay."

The look on his face wasn't discernible and she couldn't't see how he felt. She opened her mouth to protest, but he cut her off. "Don't even go there. I'll be back at one, be ready."

He walked to his truck got in and drove off
waving to her. She just stood, stunned, wondering
what was going to happen to her. She was feeling
things she thought she would never feel again.
Again? Who the hell was she fooling? She had
never felt like this. The feelings racing through her
were for a man she wasn't married to and who was
married to someone else. She was in trouble in a
way she couldn't define. Strangely she was looking
forward to the trouble.

When Ty came to her office, she tried to insist
on following him in her car but he wouldn't hear
of it.

"I'm taking you to lunch and that's that."
The strong black man thing was becoming more
and more appealing.

When she got into his truck, she was excited,
like she was going on her first date and trying real
hard not to show it. They drove for about an hour.
She realized they had driven to the woods and
were at a restaurant she had heard about, but never
patronized. It was a restaurant/hotel and was built
on a manmade peninsula, very beautiful, peaceful
and secluded. When they got inside it was even
more beautiful, very cozy and intimate. It was
furnished with dark wood and leather, and had soft
beige lighting. She was scared out of her wits. She
had not been alone with a man other than Wayne
or a relative in over thirteen years. Not even for a
conversation and now she was here in some

restaurant that looked like a lover's hideaway. She was with a man she had only known for a few days, hours if you really counted it up. He had already told her what he was going to do to her and she knew her life was going to change in ways she had never even thought of. She wanted to pour the pitcher of cold water all over her body. She was so heated.

They ordered lunch and talked. He asked about her life, her family and her marriage. Amazingly she told him and she told him the truth, which really surprised her because she usually pretended all was well.

"I knew you were love starved when I met you. That's a damn shame. You are too beautiful for that. Every woman deserves to be loved fully and often."

She could feel heat in her loins and chest. She squeezed her legs together hoping that would help. She shoveled crab salad into her mouth. She figured if her mouth were full, she wouldn't have to talk. Tyrone waited a minute, he then continued talking.

"My wife and I have an open marriage. Neither of us thinks it is possible to be sexually faithful forever. We discreetly do our thing with no questions asked. We make sure to protect and respect each other, or at least we did."

He paused for effect, noticing her mouth hanging open in shock.

"My wife changed the game. She decided to fall in love with her lover. Now she wants out of the marriage."

He shook his head as though he couldn't believe it.

Glo was so amazed she didn't know how to respond. After several minutes she asked, "What are you going to do?"

"I'm going to let her go. That house is for her and my boys. I can deal with her having sex with someone else. Falling in love however, was not an option. That affects our lives. She is staying out nights and refusing me my rights. She has to go." He looked at Glo for a minute. What an arrogant man. He continued talking.

"I knew the games were over because we agreed years ago that if the rules were broken we would move on. I'm giving her the house and two hundred thousand. I'll keep seven hundred thousand and six will be invested for my boys. The boys are fifteen and sixteen and we *will* share custody. Checkmate, game over." That sounded so damn cold and calculated to Glo.

Ty knew Glo couldn't believe people actually lived like he and Veronica did. He knew she felt she could never do it, but she would find out that everyone is capable of a lot of different things. They finished their meals and he paid the check. When they stood up he looked down into her innocent brown eyes.

"Come on let me take you back to work, before you turn into a pumpkin or lose your glass slipper." He knew she wasn't ready for him yet, but he was patient and would wait until she was.

Over the next few weeks, Glo was very busy. Once word was out about her big sale, she was in demand. Ty had been phoning her regularly and had taken her to lunch a few times. She was becoming more and more attracted to him. Mostly she loved talking to him. He made her laugh and think. The lunches were always romantic and well thought out. She *was* love and attention starved. She didn't know what she was going to do. Her course of action was decided for her, by one conversation with her husband.

Wayne came home from work one evening, announcing he wanted to talk. She was shocked because Wayne never wanted to talk about anything. At least not with her, he talked with Maya all the time and she assumed with his coworkers. He went to work, came home, ate dinner, spent time with Maya, and had antiseptic sex with Glo every few weeks. He spent increasing amounts of time with his friends playing golf or whatever it was they did.

After dinner, when Maya had gone next door to talk to her friends, they sat down on the porch.

"Gloria, are you happy?" Wayne asked a question that had never crossed his lips, at least not to her. Glo was more surprised by the question than she was by the fact they were talking.

"As happy as I know how to be."
He looked at her with tears pooling in his eyes.
Glo realized Wayne was still a handsome man. She
hadn't really looked at him in years. He was tall,
very slender with light brown eyes and toffee
colored skin. He was always immaculately dressed
and groomed.

"Gloria we are pretty pathetic. I love you and
Maya but I have never been in love with you. I
have never felt passion in our marriage. We have
always just gone by the motions. I know you are
not in love with me, either."

Glo just listened to what he was saying, she
knew there had to be more to this than had already
been said. He then dropped his bombshell.

"I think I may be bisexual. I have wondered for
years. I have been married to a beautiful, sexy
woman and have never really connected with her."

Glo thought, *"Now when he tells me he prefers
penises, I am beautiful and sexy."* After pausing
for a reaction, he didn't receive, Wayne continued.
"I have found myself attracted to a man in my
office. For the past couple of months he seems to
be on my mind more than he should be. We
haven't done anything yet, but I know we're going
to and I want you to know." He said all of this in a
monotone, as though talking about the weather.

All Glo could think was, *"I should certainly feel
more than I am feeling, I should act surprised or
something. Maybe I should be screaming or hitting
him."* She didn't feel anything, except a strange

kind of relief. She was grateful he had been honest with her, before he'd done something.

She stood, strolling towards the bedroom; she didn't want to talk any longer. There really was nothing to say. She couldn't shake the feeling she should be doing something, crying, cussing, something. But she simply continued walking away from him. Almost as an afterthought she told him, "Please find you someplace to live Wayne, also come up with a way to tell Maya, and make sure you don't hurt her. I am very tired and need a nap." She continued to the bedroom, never once looking back.

When she woke up she discovered Wayne was gone. His bedside table was empty, as was his side of the closet. He left a note telling her he was glad she understood and that he would be staying at the Radisson until he could find somewhere permanent to stay. The note also said he would continue to pay the mortgage, and would send her money for Maya.

He was a decent man and a good father, she expected no less from him. He wrote that he didn't want to think about divorce because he wanted to keep his family.

Glo smiled sadly, she knew she wasn't going to allow that to happen. She was going to divorce him because she wanted to find some happiness and passion for herself. She needed to be free to do that. It was almost as if she had been waiting for him to make the decision. Most importantly, she wasn't going to allow Wayne's lifestyle to touch or affect Maya. Their daughter was her main concern. She walked downstairs and saw Maya eating cereal at the kitchen counter. She looked at her to see if she were okay. Maya was a combination of the two of them. She was tall and thin like her dad, but had her mom's pecan brown skin, thick hair and dreamy brown eyes. Glo's heart filled with love, she was glad that she and Wayne had created such an awesome child.

Before Glo could say a word, Maya surprised her.

"Hey Ma, I want you to know I understand why daddy is going away, you all are sooooo boring together." She hugged her mama to her. "I told daddy that I want both of you to be happy."

Glo was surprised at how mature her baby sounded. "What else did daddy say?"

"Not much, just that ya'll need some time apart."

Glo was grateful for how Wayne had handled it, but Maya needed to know that it was more than just a separation.

"Baby it's more than time apart, daddy and I are going to get a divorce."

"Ma I think I knew that, I know you both love me. I just want to spend time with you and my daddy." Glo smiled at that, her heart was full. It was good to know how much Maya loved them both.

"Boo Boo, that's the way it should be and it will be."
She pulled Maya into her arms and hugged her, kissing her on her forehead. She could smell mango shampoo and captain crunch cereal.

Then like a typical thirteen-year-old, Maya asked if she could go to the movies with her friends and spend the night with one of them. Glo smiled, nodding affirmatively. She looked forward to some time to think and to spending what would be the first night in life, alone. She felt somewhat scared but exhilarated at the same time.

The next few days went ok. There were some times when Glo felt sad for all the time she had wasted and other days she was just glad it was over. She even felt angry, wanting to blame Wayne. She knew though there was really no one to blame. They had been equally responsible for staying in a cold loveless marriage.

Glo told her parents and of course they didn't agree with her decision to get a divorce. Her parents were old school Christians who believed you stayed married no matter what. In fact her mom's exact words had been," Gloria Denise, a part of marriage is long suffering. Marriage is not one long romantic adventure. You need to grow up. You are married to a man that provides for you and your baby. He does not hit you or abuse you. You live very well. What else do you want or need?" There were a few things that Glo could have said but she knew that would have been pointless.

Glo knew that even if she had told her mom and dad all of the details, they would still have told her to pray and make the best of it. She knew she could pray until she was blue in the face and her knees were sore, now that Wayne had told her he was going to do his thing, nothing was going to change. Praying wasn't going to make him love her or make her love him. She had been praying for that for years.

After Wayne had been gone for a few weeks, Ty stopped by her office to invite her to dinner. She had spoken to him a few times since the separation but hadn't discussed her personal business. She had not asked him about his status with Mrs. Williams either.

"I won't be done here until seven. Is that too late for dinner, Mister?" Glo was seriously flirting now, testing her man-getting skills.

"That is fine with me. How will your man feel about you being out that late?"

"He will be alright, pick me up at seven. You worry about Veronica." She rolled her big brown eyes for effect.

He chuckled, she blushed and a spontaneous giggle burst out of her.

"See you at seven."

He arrived promptly at seven.

"Do you want to go back to the woods?"

"Yes, I do, that would be nice." She looked straight in his face. He looked back at her for several long minutes.

"You look different, freer or something." She didn't reply. She grabbed her purse, strutting outside. She was wearing a new snug lavender pantsuit and she knew it showed off all of her assets. She also knew he was checking them out.

During the drive to the woods, she told him about her separation. She told him all of the details. He listened, which was something, she really liked about him. He always listened like what she had to say was important. He was a very seductive man.

"Please don't feel like you did anything wrong. When a brother has interests like that, there is nothing a sister can do to change it. At least he showed some honor by telling you what was up, most of the time it's done behind your back. That's why I'm upfront about what I do. That sure explains why your beautiful eyes are always so sad. By the way, Veronica and I are separated also. We have filed for a divorce and she's going to marry her lover. I give that marriage a year, two years top. I'm chilling right now. I'm not seeing anyone. I love marriage. I will just have to make sure that my next wife understands the game." Glo could feel his eyes on her but she looked out the window.

"I will love and cherish my wife and fulfill her heart's desires. I will just occasionally have sex with other women. She can also do her thing. What she can't do is mess up the main relationship." His voice was so damn seductive. He sounded so sincere with his BS.

Glo did not agree, but she could see how he could feel the way he did. Everyone she knew had cheated on their spouses, or had something on the side. Ironically, she and Wayne were the only people she knew who were as miserable as they were and had stayed faithful sexually.

When they got to the restaurant, Ty told her to wait in the car because he was going to change the reservations. When he came back he drove her to the end of the complex and stopped at one of the rooms. Glo looked at him with fear in her eyes. He laughed quietly.

"Relax baby, we will have dinner in the room. I have no expectations. If you decide to try something with me, I might let you."
He laughed again as he walked around to open her door. Ty was ridiculous with his arrogance. Glo loved it.

She got out of the care, strolling inside with him. The room was huge and very nice. It was one big, wide, open space. There was a huge bed covered with chocolate colored silk sheets, a fireplace, a hot tub and a little dining area in the corner. There was a door leading to the balcony and another door leading to what had to be the bathroom.

Ty immediately took off his shoes and socks. He pulled his shirt out of his pants and sat down on the floor. She was nervous, so she told him she had to use the bathroom. When she came out, the waiter had delivered the food. Teddy Pendergrass was playing in the background, and the fireplace was lit.

She kicked off her shoes, sitting down on the floor next to Ty. She was trying to be spontaneous. Spontaneity was totally out of character for her. She had promised herself she would try as hard as she could to live in the moment and to make sure her own needs were met. She knew she wanted to be close to Ty. She wasn't sure where things would go or if they could go anywhere at all because she certainly didn't agree with his ideas on marriage. She wanted and needed to feel like a desirable woman and right now Ty had her wide open to that. They ate the dinner, drank wine and talked about dreams and desires. She was totally relaxed for a change.

"Have you ever been loved properly, Gloria?" His voice was as silky and dark as those sheets on the bed.

"Define properly." Her voice was shaking.

'Do you know what it is like to *know* your man wakes up with you on his mind, the taste of you on his tongue? Have you ever had the knowledge that no matter what he does you are the center of his world? Have you ever been licked from the top of your head to the tips of your toes? Has anyone ever gotten up in the middle of the night to get you a glass of water with freshly squeezed lemon just because you were thirsty? Or rubbed your back and neck for so long that your whole body relaxes?"

She was so overwhelmed with desire and the picture he had painted in her mind she could only shake her head.

"That will be my mission sweet, sexy Gloria. I only just met you but you are already in my blood. I will love you the way you deserve to be loved." He leaned over, licking her lips, pulling them into his mouth. The mixture of intense pleasure and slight pain caused liquid heat to run through her veins.

To create a distraction she asked, "Is that how you treated your wife?"

"Absolutely, and the way I would still treat her and love her if she hadn't changed up on me. She foolishly came to the conclusion that love and sex are the same. I don't agree, so we can't be together, that would create too much drama. Tyrone Williams does not do drama."

Glo stared at him. She knew she didn't believe in his way of living, but what she did know was she really wanted some of him. She wanted him to lick her lips again. Since she wasn't in love with him now, she figured she could stop herself from ever being in love with him.

That night, the process of wooing Glo began. Ty did all the things he had described. He kissed and licked her from head to toe. He made love to her whole body and engaged her mind. He even talked to her while he was making love to her. He told her exactly what he was going to do to her, while he did it. He knew how to make love to a woman. Glo was one totally, sexually satisfied woman by the time she left that room. She knew she wanted more, more, and more. She'd made love back to him. She had never kissed a man anywhere except his mouth. Tyrone had felt her lips and tongue all over his body. She couldn't't wait to love him again. In the back of her mind she was already thinking what had gotten women in trouble since then beginning of time. "I know he will change for me. I will be the one to turn him around."

Driving back to town she sat close to him in the seat.

"I want to see you Glo, be with you. I'm not with anyone right now but you. If that changes, you will be the first to know."

She was so caught up in the afterglow of their lovemaking she smiled her acceptance.

"We are just fooling around right now. I have no strings on you Tyrone."

"Woman, yes you do. You just wrapped some serious strings around me. So, I am telling you how I roll. You will always know what is what. I expect the same from you."

She nodded again, thinking, "I will never get to the place where I am sexing more than one man at any given time." Right then, her heart wasn't completely involved. She had just been made love to by an extraordinarily skilled lover. She loved it and she wanted more.

Over the next few months, Glo and Wayne divorced in a user-friendly way, no drama. Maya seemed untouched by what was going on because she was enjoying being a teenager. She had the love of her parents. They were both at her beck and call. Glo didn't know exactly what Wayne had told her, but she knew it was up to him to tell Maya not her. She would only have to be there to pick up the pieces if the story came out negatively. She wasn't overly concerned about that though because Wayne was very conservative. He would make sure no one knew, except people he wanted to know. He worshipped the ground his baby girl walked on and would do nothing to hurt her.

Ty and Veronica were finalizing their divorce deal. There had been a bit of a problem about money at the last minute. Veronica felt she should get more money and the house because the boys were living with her. Ty made sure she knew the six hundred thousand was for the boys. The interest alone would take care of them annually, until the funds were available to them. Finally, she accepted, she had gotten the deal she had originally asked for.

Ty suspected her new man had encouraged her to ask for more, but he had figured that in when the deal was made. Glo realized Ty was one of the smartest and most calculating people she had ever met. The people who chose not to play by his rules would probably not get to play.

She was so sexed up and romanced she wasn't thinking about any of that. All she knew and cared about at the time was that she was getting treated special. Not to mention getting the best loving she'd ever had. He was taking her to nice restaurants. He was massaging her neck and back and even painting her toenails. Flowers and perfume were coming in the door regularly, so she wasn't tripping about anything else. And the sex left her speechless. She had fallen in love and Ty had told her he was in love with her too. Her mind and body were not allowing her to think beyond what she was feeling. For the first time in her life, she was really feeling and just going with the flow. Ty was the center of her universe.

By the time Glo and Ty had been dating for a year, he had asked her to marry him. She was hesitant because she knew his ideas on fidelity hadn't changed in any form or fashion. She was not surprised when he proposed to her.

"Baby in the year that we have been together, I have never been with another woman. I have not even wanted to. I'm currently not even looking for that. I have met many women that were attractive and attracted to me. I want you to be my wife, I love you."

"What about other women, later?"

"What about them? If you're asking will I ever be with another woman, the answer is probably." Her heart fluttered in her chest.

"I don't know if I can deal with the idea of that, you making love to another woman. How can you stand the thought of another man making love to me?" He reached for her. She swatted his hand away.

"Baby love is what you feel in your heart and soul and how you treat people. Sex is feeling with your body, period. Most adults know that to be true, but because of religious or perceived moral ideas, they never admit it even to themselves."

Glo knew intellectually he might be right, but she also knew she didn't want to spend her life thinking of Ty doing to other women what he did to her. She didn't expect to do that with anyone else or risk exposing him to something.

When she verbalized this to him, he said, "Of course you are right. Neither one of us would have unsafe sex with another person. You are the only woman I have never used a condom with. I even used one with Veronica, except to get her pregnant. I don't expect you to do anything with another man that would expose me to anything. I won't do anything with another woman that would expose you. Baby we are talking straight up sexual intercourse here. We both know to save the freaky sexual behavior for within the marriage. I don't even kiss women I'm not in love with. She gets hers, I get mine, and we move on."

Glo shook her head because she knew she would never feel like he did. Yet, she wanted to marry Ty so bad. Her female ego was still telling her she could be the only love and lover in his life.

After a few weeks of thought, she decided she would rather be with him on his terms than be without him on any terms. Her fate was sealed. They told the kids, who had already become close, and their respective families. Everyone seemed happy for them. All of Glo's family and friends had noticed how happy and carefree she had become in the past year. They also noticed how much younger she looked and how she laughed and joked more often. Ty's family seemed happy too, they were a bit more reserved because they knew him. They wondered if Glo was up to the challenge. Ty was a known entity to his family. There was no shame in his game. He was just Ty.

For the first couple of years, things were beautiful. They built their dream home and combined their families. Glo got pregnant within months. They had a daughter, named Sanaa. They were just doing the things that young, happy, upwardly mobile folks do. But one day into the third year of marriage, Ty told Glo he was going to dinner with a client and would be home late. There was something about the way he said client that made the hair stand up on the back of her neck.

"When did you start going to dinner with clients?"

"Tonight, I could give you the details if you want them but I feel you would prefer not to know." His eyes were fastened on hers.

Her heart almost stopped beating because she knew what that meant. She just looked at him with fear in her eyes, pain in her heart.

"Is there anything I can do to make you change your mind?"

"No baby, not a thing. This is just Ty being Ty." She hated when he said that. "It will not affect you or our lives in any way unless you allow it to. You know you have options as well."

"So I don't appeal to you anymore?"

"Baby, that has nothing to do with this, nothing at all. You are the most appealing woman in the world." He took her in his arms, holding her close.

"Do you feel the way my heart is beating when I hold you. Nothing and no one will ever come between that." Those words did not stop him from walking out the door.

When he left, Glo felt like hell, she didn't know what he was doing. All night long she wondered about Ty being with someone else. Glo worried about all the things women worry about. Was the other woman prettier, finer, or sexier? Would she make Ty love her?" She felt crushed by the pain of knowing Ty was having sex with another woman.

She finally fell into a fitful sleep. She was awakened at about two a.m., to the sound of Ty coming in the room. She heard him use the toilet and flush. He washed his hands, she listened for the shower but it never came on.

When he came into the room, he took off all of his clothes the way he always did, dropping them on the floor beside the bed. He got in behind her and took her in his arms the way he always did. She was so tense and filled with pain.

"Relax baby. I love you sweet Gloria." He kissed her neck and within minutes he was snoring gently with her wrapped in his arms.

She lay there with her mind all over the place. All she could think was that he smelled just like the soap and cologne, he always used. There was not a mark on his body that indicated anything. She prayed, *"Lord what in the world am I going to do? This is killing me."* She silently cried herself to sleep.

The next morning she woke up to Ty kissing her stomach. She badly wanted to resist him, but she didn't have the ability to do that. He was making love to her as only he could. He was kissing the thoughts of what he had done the night before right out of her mind. When he was done loving her, he said, "Baby you are my love, and always will be."

She didn't say a word because she had a huge lump in her throat. She feared the lump would choke her to death. Ty got up and went downstairs to make her breakfast. He brought the bacon, toast and coffee and served it to her in bed. After eating she continued to lie there watching him get ready for work. He came over to tell her he was leaving.

"Baby I'm going now, I will be home on time tonight. Maybe we can go out for dinner, or if you want I can bring something in." He looked down at her waiting for a response.

"Whatever Tyrone, whatever you say." He leaned over, kissing her lightly. Lying in her bed she realized that as painful as this shit was, she could probably learn to live with it. She didn't want to lose her man. Turning her back to him she said, "No more advance notices, I can't take that."

"Okay baby, but when you step out I want to know. That is a one-time request." His voice was quiet and serious.

"That will never happen." She spoke those words with conviction. She really believed what she was saying.

He smiled, "Whatever you say baby." He kissed her again on the mouth and nose and walked out of the bedroom, gently closing the door behind him. When she got up, she picked his clothes up from the floor. She placed them to her nose and the only scents were of Ty and Polo cologne. There was no lipstick on his collar and no phone numbers in his pockets. If he hadn't told her she would have never known.

Ty and Glo were married for five years before it ever occurred to her to even consider the possibility of being with someone else. She knew Ty'd had a couple of "clients" over the past couple of years. It had never particularly affected them beyond the fact that she knew. When he was seeing clients, he would be out late at least one day every couple of weeks. This would last for a couple of months. There would be months with no routine changes and then it would start again. She had come to recognize the pattern.

The way he treated her or the regularity of their lovemaking or the romantic and thoughtful things he did never changed. Most surprisingly, she had never heard a word. They had a pretty large circle of acquaintances and no one had ever said a word to her about Ty or any of his activities. In fact, most people commented on how good she had it, how much he loved her, and how well he treated her.

Right before Glo's fortieth birthday, she started doubting herself and her attractiveness. She spent too much time wondering if the women her husband was spending time with were younger, smarter or prettier than she. All of the shit that aging women take themselves through, particularly if they know their man is cheating. Ty, of course would not ever have *that* discussion with her. His words were always the same.

"Baby I love you more than ever. You are the only woman I love. You are more beautiful than you were all those years ago when I first saw you. No woman on earth can take your place. She didn't believe him, because she knew how much he'd loved his first wife.

That was a part of the problem because she knew Veronica was back on the market. Her second marriage had ended, just as Ty had predicted, after a couple of years. Nothing Ty ever said indicated he was seeing Veronica, and Glo knew he wouldn't tell her, it just wasn't his way. It was not one of the rules. Her fears were based on how honest he had been from the start about how much he had loved Veronica. Glo knew Ty only married women he adored and who turned him inside out, which made her even less secure. He had just been too damn honest.

Veronica was three years older than Glo, but she still looked amazing. Glo was jealous of her. Ironically, she was not jealous of the others but the ex-wife was driving her crazy. Glo felt she was not only getting old, but she was also losing her mind.

Right in the nick of time a new, younger guy came to work for her agency. The new guy forced her to change her mind about everything she had thought about herself. The first time Glo saw Jamal she thought, *"Wow, what a fine young man that is if he were a little younger he would be a great catch for Maya."*

He was thirty years old and had that smooth brother, hip-hop thing going on. He was bald and dressed very trendy, but with a conservative bent. He would wear ultra- conservative suits with funky colored shirts, or boots instead of regular shoes, or jeans with tuxedo jackets and conservative shoes. He was quite tall, lean and dark-skinned, a totally different look from the other men who had been in her life. He had an extraordinary, laid back, yet ambitious demeanor that seemed to personify younger men who knew they were going places. He was also very afro-centric.

When he was introduced to her, she was told he would be on her team. He had come from a sister real estate agency and had a reputation for being able to sell anything to anyone.

"Jamal I hear you are a burner, when it comes to sales." He looked at her and smiled.

"Yep, that's how I do it." He had the audacity to wink at her.

She felt silly because she was grinning back at this kid like she was crazy. She had a twenty year old daughter and should know better. The first couple of weeks he was in the office they attended meetings and he was getting to know the other players. But, on the third week, she knew it was time to take him in the field and show him some of the properties they had for sale or the ones they would like to get. She insisted on driving because that allowed her to stay in control of the situation. They had small talk for most of the morning and she told him about her daughters and stepsons. He talked about his parents and siblings. Finally, he turned the conversation more personal.

"How long have you been married, because anyone with a rock the size of the one on your finger, has to have been married a long time?"

"I have been married currently, for almost six years. I was married before, for over thirteen years."

"Damn, you look young! You look way too young to have been collectively married for twenty years. Wow!"

"I am forty years old."

"Well, you certainly look younger than that but you *are* too young to have been married twenty years. You didn't even have a chance to live before you got married."

"Of course I lived. I just haven't been like a lot of people my age and younger, jumping in an out of beds and exposing myself to diseases and stuff."

He laughed, everything seemed funny to his young ass.

"Touche', you are right about that, but I still think no one should get married before age thirty, thirty-five for men. That way once you are married, you will have gotten all that player, player shit out of your system."

"Is it out of yours? I have a daughter I might introduce you to if you are done playing."

He looked at her in a strange way, very focused.

"I'm not really done yet. I figure I still got a

couple of years. Besides, I'm not interested in meeting your daughter because I don't date women when I'm already interested in their mamas."

The car went dead silent. She focused on driving. She didn't have a response to that. He was not sure why he'd said that. He knew she was married but he felt the need to put his feelings out there. The remainder of the afternoon they talked about work-related topics and avoided the personal. His comments played over and over again in her mind.

A couple of weeks later, Jamal got the opportunity to meet Ty. About once a year Glo threw a party at their home for her team. Ty liked doing it and showing off his cooking skills. Jamal brought a woman, who he introduced to everyone as a friend. Glo immediately noticed she was older than him, not as old as her, but a good five years older than Jamal. Glo was real intrigued by that, fascinated in fact. The party went well, Ty played the gracious host. He was very good at putting people at ease.

At the end of the night when they were cleaning up, Ty started questioning her.

"Hey baby, why no mention that you had a new team member?" Glo immediately felt defensive.

"I am sure I told you."

"No, you told me you were getting one, not that you had one. In the past, you have always told me when someone joined the team or someone left. What's up with this one?"

"Nothing! Why are you asking all of these questions?"

"Pump the breaks baby, no need to get attitude. The deal is that I can tell young Jamal wants my wife. His eyes were on you all night long. I think you are feeling his young ass too. I don't have a problem with any of that, if it is about getting some. But, *we will* have a problem if you are trying to have him fall in love with you or vice versa." He continued to sweep the floor nonchalantly, but his voice was serious. She turned around from the sink, looking at him in surprise.

"I didn't think you cared about that."

"Damn right, I care. You can sex if you want to, but you can't have relationships, that was made clear years ago. His being so young is a problem, young brothers these days are always trying to take it to the next level. The fact that he's single could be a problem. I should have told you single men were off limits. That's exactly what happened with Veronica."

"Don't even compare us! She and I are nothing alike. She's more like you, than I will ever be. You have been out there for years and I have done nothing. She was out there with you from the minute you guys got married, so our situation isn't the same. Jamal works for and with me, end of story." She was slamming dishes inside the cabinet she was so agitated.

"No it is worse *because* you have done nothing. The chance of you thinking it's something it isn't is greater, if it happened to her, you are damn sure at risk. She was a player from the starting line, you are not." Glo was surprised at the heat in his voice. Ty was usually as cool as popsicles.

"I am done talking about this Tyrone Williams."

"Okay, but you had better know that you and I are going to stay together. You can step out, but you can't stay out. I will reel you back in. We are going to raise Sanaa together and stay married."

"Are you jealous?" She wanted him to say yes so badly.

"Not jealous, just cautious, I guess I just never thought you were going to go out there. I fell into a comfort zone and now I don't know what I'm feeling. I'm not trying to change the game, just reinforce the rules."

They stood facing each other. Glo thought, "He's being way too honest and too controlling." He leaned over, kissing her on the nose and walked from the room.

The next time she saw Jamal he wanted to talk about Ty. "Your husband didn't seem to like me."

"He didn't like you or dislike you. Ty does not waste energy on that kind of thing. He thinks you want me."

"Your husband is a very insightful man. There is nothing I want more than to have your legs wrapped around me and having you scream my name at the top of your lungs. I do want you." He was matter-of-fact about it. She walked away.

She avoided being alone with him over the next few weeks. After a while, she couldn't't avoid him because they had to show a house together. The rest as they say was history. The house for the showing was one of the exhibition homes, the last one to be sold. Once they had shown the house and the last client had left, it started raining. They were stuck in the house. Glo was pacing around the house praying for the rain to stop. Before she could stop him, Jamal walked up to her and placed his lips on hers, she kissed him back. Her body responded to the different way he had of touching her. Without one word of protest from her, he undressed her. In minutes they were on the floor, naked in front of the fireplace. He made love to her in the way only a young man can, over and over again. The lovemaking was so good and so different. Most importantly it was "just sex". She wasn't in love with Jamal. She just wanted him.
There was this song playing in her mind of what she should be doing and allowing him to do, but the song grew fainter and fainter as he continued making love to her. Jamal didn't know what the rules were, so he was creating his own.

A few hours later, after the rain had stopped, they packed up and left. She dropped him off at the agency then drove home. She couldn't stop thinking, *"I just had sex with someone who is not my husband. And damn it was good."* Tremors were running through her thinking about how he had made her feel.

"It won't happen again." Glo knew she was lying to herself. She picked up Sanaa and went home, took a shower, cooked dinner and played with her daughter. She froze when she heard Ty come in the door.

"Hey, baby." She got up and walked into his arms, her heart was racing.

"You okay?" Ty pulled back a bit to look at her.

"I'm fine, just tired. After dinner I'm going to take a nap. I have been real busy this week, with three closings."

"Hey, why don't you just go upstairs, take a nap, I will feed Sanaa and myself. I will be up to check on you later."

"Are you sure? That would be good, I'm not very hungry."

"Yeah baby, I got it." He kissed her on the lips. She could feel his eyes on her as she walked out of the room. The guilt had finally taken hold of her. She took three Tylenol pm, got in the bed and fell asleep until the morning. When she woke up Ty was sitting on the side of the bed looking at her.

"Do you feel better? Is there anything you want to talk about?"

"I'm fine, I just needed some rest. I love you."

"I love you too baby. Will you be home when I get home tonight?"

"Of course, Sanaa is going to Mama's, it will just be us." She looked at him. His face was guarded. "Good, we can use some time alone." He kissed her, got up and left the room. She got up to prepare for the day. She didn't want to think about what had happened yesterday.

Glo and Jamal had four other encounters, but it was too much for both of them. For Glo it was the working together aspect and the knowledge that she had no feelings for him beyond sexual desire. Jamal was struggling with her being married and his heart was getting involved. She was feeling guilty and he was starting to feel hurt, Jamal was a "guilty pleasure" for her, she was special to him.

After a couple of months they agreed to end it, he came to her office one afternoon, closing the door behind him, standing, refusing to take a seat.

"Gloria I would appreciate it if you would help me transfer to the office across town."

"That's best for both of us. I'm sorry I allowed this to happen. I knew better. I care about your feelings and I should have never gone there."

"You care about my feelings, but not about me, right?"

"Jamal this is best for all parties." She didn't answer his question.

A couple weeks after Jamal transferred, Ty asked her, "Are you okay now that your little fling is over?"

"You knew?" Surprise was clear in her voice. She thought she'd been so careful.

"Of course, I knew the same way you know. I'm cool, if it's done."

"It is", she sighed. She felt stupid and ashamed talking about this with her husband. She wondered if he'd had her followed. That wouldn't surprise her.

"Baby, you know I love you and I know you love me. None of this shit can touch us." He took a sip of brandy, his attention focused on her. She remained silent and thought, *"I hope so, because I love you so much and want to stay married."*

Over the next nine years, Glo had a few more flings she made sure she didn't work with them. All of them ended the same way the one with Jamal had, a couple of times and then it was over. Their lives had turned out just as Ty had predicted.

She knew that over the years Ty'd had several "clients" and was involved with someone now, nothing had changed in their lives, except for the fact that Glo was changing. At her age she knew she wasn't interested in taking her clothes off for another man. She also knew that while she'd had good sex with a handful of people it couldn't compare to making love while in love. Ty was the best love she had ever made. She was tired. She was also spiritually bankrupt, she felt like a hypocrite.

Ty was fifty-three and as virile as ever. She didn't know how he felt about any of this anymore because they hadn't discussed any of it since the Jamal situation. Glo knew it was time to talk.

Glo called her sex partner and told him she was going to cancel. She was burning a bridge. But, that was okay it was a bridge she no longer had an interest in crossing.

She was sitting in the living room waiting for Ty when he walked in the door.

"Husband, we need to talk."

"Do I need to sit for this or continue standing?" Something that sounded akin to fear was in his voice.

"Sitting would work best." He sat down across from her.

"What is this all about, Glo? I'm surprised to see you sitting here. Don't you have plans tonight?"

"I did, but I decided I don't want to do it anymore."

"Do what?" There was definitely fear in his voice.

"Tyrone, I'm no longer interested in sexing people I don't love, so I can stay with someone I do. I'm also tired of knowing that at least three

months out of every year my husband, the man I love is out sexing someone else. The whole thing has just started to funk up my mind. It disgusts me! I disgust me! You disgust me! I'm so afraid I'm going to be in church or showing a house and some man who has seen me naked will show up."
Tyrone flinched at the remark.

"Have you fallen in love with someone Glo, or fallen out of love with me?" His voice was low and controlled.

"Negro, please! If that were true I would leave your ass. I'm almost fifty years old and I know God doesn't want my married, old ass jumping in and out of beds. Most importantly, I don't want it. I spent thirteen years married to a sissy and the last fifteen married to a whore. I have become a whore myself and I just *will not* live like this, any longer." Tyrone moved over to the couch next to her. A look of relief was evident in his eyes. The look of relief surprised her.

"You know I want to give you everything you want. Baby, don't think for a minute that I don't get tired, but I have spent my life trying not to love anything too much. I failed that when I met you. My dad raised me to believe that a black man should work hard, marry a pretty woman, raise responsible kids and always have something on the side. He did and my mom adored him. I have spent my life believing his words, and living my life like that. I can admit that it has almost killed me thinking about you with other men. Way back when you were messing with that young boy, that shit almost drove me crazy. I remember seeing you sit there with Sanaa; your skin was all aglow. I knew that only one thing produced that look in you. I wanted to kill him. But I set all of that up, because that was my history, what I believed. I felt entitled to have other women. For over six years you were faithful to me. I thought you would never step out, and then one day you did. So, I convinced myself that every one of us was the same and that you were no different. We were just doing our thing. I have never been happy about you being with anyone."

Tears were streaming down Glo's face.

"Why didn't you tell me all this years ago? Before I sold my soul to the devil! Ty, how could you?" He shook his head miserably, fighting to hold back his own tears. She wanted to slap him.

"I didn't have the right to because by the time you got out there I had been out there for years and it was my game. I couldn't show weakness or be a hypocrite. I just had to let the shit play out. As I told you then, I will never let you go. I am willing to try to do whatever it takes to make this work. Don't leave me." His voice cracked with emotion. "I know my ass is getting old and I have always known that pussy is just pussy unless you love what goes with it. I just felt that as a man, extra pussy was just something I was entitled to." He laughed bitterly at the absurdity of that statement.

Glo thought of all the unnecessary pain they had caused each other, and for what? She closed her eyes, praying. She prayed that even though they had lived separate love lives for so long, maybe they still had a chance to have just one love life. Ty was lost in his own thoughts. She reached for her husband's hand. He held on with everything in him.

Glo and Ty were silent as they made their way to their bedroom and went through their bedtime rituals. Once they were in bed, Ty wrapped himself around her.

"Gloria Williams, I have loved you always. I will love you always."

"I love you, Tyrone Williams."

Soon, they were both snoring gently.

www.ingramcontent.com/pod-product-compliance
Lightning Source LLC
Chambersburg PA
CBHW020955160726
47994CB00006B/2230